Don Nehlen's

TALES FROM THE WEST VIRGINIA SIDELINE

Don Nehlen
with Shelly Poe

SPORTS PUBLISHING L.L.C.

SportsPublishingLLC.com

Photos courtesy of West Virginia Sports Communications, the Nehlen Family Collection, and Chyleen Young.

Publishers: Peter L. Bannon and Joseph J. Bannon Sr.
Senior managing editor: Susan M. Moyer
Acquisitions editor: John Humenik
Developmental editor: Suzanne E. Perkins
Art director: K. Jeffrey Higgerson
Dust jacket design: Dustin Hubbart
Interior layout: Kathryn R. Holleman
Photo editor: Erin Linden-Levy

Printed in the United States of America

Sports Publishing L.L.C.
804 North Neil Street
Champaign, IL 61820
Phone: 1-877-424-2665
Fax: 217-363-2073
SportsPublishingLLC.com

Library of Congress Cataloging-in-Publication Data

Nehlen, Don.
  Don Nehlen's tales from the West Virginia sideline / Don Nehlen with Shelly Poe.
    p. cm.
  ISBN 1-59670-022-X (hard copy : alk. paper)
  1. West Virginia University--Football. 2. West Virginia Mountaineers (Football Team) 3. Nehlen, Don. 4. Football coaches--United States. I. Poe, Shelly, 1964- II. Title. III. Title: Tales from the West Virginia sideline.

GV958.W4N44 2006
796.332'630975452--dc22
                                    2006019058

CONTENTS

FOREWORD

Being a part of the winning team in Super Bowl XL was the realization of a dream, and being a Super Bowl champion with my hometown Pittsburgh Steelers is beyond description. During Super Bowl week, I spent some time reflecting. So many people contributed to my success, but right at the top of the list is Don Nehlen. What an amazing guy! I still picture the first time I met him: those piercing blue eyes, that infectious grin, and that very crooked index finger. On my recruiting visit, he stuck his hand out to seal the deal, and all I could see was that finger. I know I looked at him with some uncertainty. Coach laughed and explained how his finger had been broken. It's ironic that I remember that—after all my football injuries, my finger today doesn't look much better!

At the end of my freshman year, I went in Coach's office for that annual see-where-you-stand talk. It was my first time, and I was nervous. Some of the upperclassmen had told me, "If he looks out the window, then he might not be too serious about you." With that in mind, I sat down across the desk and looked Coach Nehlen straight in the eye. Our discussion was going well, but toward the middle, his gaze started wandering, and that bothered me. I kept moving my chair toward the window to ensure he was talking directly to me. I really wanted to be one of those special guys. He gave you the encouragement to fully realize your abilities in life.

One highlight every week was at the hotel when Coach Nehlen gave his pregame speech. He had a small frame, but he got us so energized with how much he believed in us. He would ball his fist up and get so excited. His voice would go to a high pitch and he would pound the chalkboard. We believed everything he told us. We would get off that bus and play our hearts out.

As I sit back now, I see all the trials and tribulations of my football career: the injuries, adapting to different atmospheres and coaches, and accomplishing my goal of playing in the NFL. I see all the people who made it possible—too many to thank, but so many of them were at West Virginia. Coach Holmes, Coach Ramsey, Coach Kirelawich, Coach Dunlap—they were convinced I could do it. Those are the kind of people I knew at West Virginia—people who wanted you to be successful and who are rooting for me even today. I tell the guys playing at WVU now, "Don't take this for granted. You are playing in one of the greatest college atmospheres anywhere, so cherish every minute." Every time I ran out that tunnel, I felt like I was embraced by the whole state of West Virginia—like there were 200,000 people in the stadium—and I gave it my all.

Coach Nehlen brought that to West Virginia. He's an educated man, and he pushed us to graduate. He's a football man; he just wanted to play smash-mouth football, for us to do what we were taught to do and beat the other guys by doing it better. And he is very realistic about life. When I got drafted, among the abundance of advice he gave me, he told me to be smart with my money. He's a Hall of Fame coach in every sense of the term. I am so elated that I was a part of his time with West Virginia football, and I am so humbled to say Don Nehlen is my coach and my friend.

—Mike Logan
Pittsburgh Steelers

BEGINNINGS

Never while growing up did I think of being a football coach, and certainly not the head coach at a Division I school. While those things happening were surprising enough, the way I got the head coaching job at West Virginia University was nothing short of weird.

Frank Cignetti, a good man and later a friend of mine, underwent a tough battle with cancer and left the coaching position at WVU following the 1979 season. At the time, nobody in West Virginia had ever heard of Don Nehlen. Nobody. And beyond the basics of geography, I had never heard much about West Virginia either, and certainly not about West Virginia University and its football team. To be perfectly honest, it's still amazing to me that I ever became the head coach at West Virginia.

Weird, just weird. But things in football happen that way sometimes.

HOW IT ALL HAPPENED

After the 1979 regular season, I was on the way home from Cleveland, Ohio, after a recruiting trip for Michigan. I was quarterback coach for Bo Schembechler and the Wolverines, a job I'd had and loved for three years. It was Friday and I'd just gotten back when Bo called me down to his office.

I had been out on the road all week, seeing players and high school coaches and working what felt like about 65 hours straight, so I was ready to go home. I thought, "Man oh man, what in the world can he possibly want me for?"

"Boy," Bo said. He had always called me Boy or Kid since he was one of the assistant coaches when I played at Bowling Green. "Come down here. I need to talk to you." So I went down to his office.

Bo has always been a straight shooter, so he got right to the point, "Hey, are you trying to get the West Virginia job?"

He caught me completely by surprise. I wasn't aware that there was an open job at West Virginia, and I certainly had not looked into it. I said, "No," and I think Bo was surprised by my answer.

"Now wait a minute, Don—" he started, but I cut him off.

"Hey, Bo, if I was trying to get the West Virginia job, the first guy I would talk to is you," I protested. "I'm certainly not going to get any job without your help, and no, I'm not trying to get that job."

It turned out that Bo knew a lot more than I did. "A guy from West Virginia just called me, Don, and he seemed to know a lot about you," Bo said, which certainly surprised me. "I've had people talk to me about my coaches before and I've known you since you played quarterback at Bowling Green, and I'm not so sure that this guy doesn't know more about you than I do."

Bo Schembechler and me at the 1988 Doyt Perry Testimonial at Bowling Green.

The man knew about my son Danny, my daughter Vicky, my first job coaching at Mansfield High, and that I had coached at Canton South.

"It's been my experience," Bo said. "That when a guy knows as much about somebody as this guy does about you, he's obviously interested. Anyway, the guy's name is Dick Martin and he's the athletic director at West Virginia, and I'm sure he'll be getting hold of you. Are you sure you don't know Dick Martin?"

I had to admit that I'd never heard of the guy, let alone knew him, but Bo was convinced I would hear from him. He said, "I'm sure he's called you at home, because he checked your home phone number with me. I would say he's very, very interested."

When I went home, my wife, Merry Ann, mentioned that a guy named Martin from West Virginia was trying to get in touch with of me.

I told her, "Mac, that's what Bo told me. He's the athletic director at West Virginia, and their football job's open."

Merry Ann got a very puzzled look on her face. She said, "Don, I've heard of the West Virginia basketball team, with Jerry West and all, but nothing else. I don't know if West Virginia has a football team. Are you sure?"

I had to tell her, "Mac, I'm a football coach; they wouldn't be calling me about a job if they didn't have a football team."

But it did make me wonder what type of a program I might be looking into, if a football wife from Ohio had never heard of it. When I finally talked to Dick Martin, what he said jived with what Bo had told me. Martin said, "Don, I've looked around, and I'd really like to talk to you about the West Virginia job."

I told him fine. But I asked him if the job was a good one, and his answer intrigued me. Martin told me, "No, but I think it could be. Whomever we hire, we've got a new stadium planned and we're going to start to build; that's definite."

Coming off four straight losing seasons (with records of 5-6, 5-6, 2-9, and 5-6), West Virginia was preparing to move from Mountaineer Field, a 35,000-seat stadium that had been nestled in the middle of the Downtown Campus since 1924, to a new 50,000-seat facility that was being built across town on the site of the campus golf course. Many fans had opposed the new construction, preferring to renovate the ancient structure downtown, but those in favor of a new stadium had won out.

"We have a ways to go," Martin admitted. "There's no question the program now is not where we want it to be."

We agreed to meet in a few days at the Pittsburgh airport. When I got there, the place was practically deserted; there wasn't anybody around. Then Dick Martin came in with a big cowboy hat on, and

Merry Ann has been my number-one supporter throughout my entire career.

I liked him right away. We started talking and he really seemed like a good, down-to-earth guy; someone I was comfortable with. What happened next was positively amazing.

While we were talking, I looked up and the news was on the TV set. It was a Pittsburgh station and they were talking about sports. The reporter said that the West Virginia athletic director Dick Martin would be naming either Bill Mallory or Rey Dempsey as the new football coach in Morgantown within the next day or two. Martin heard it and I heard it. He was embarrassed and, of course, I was angry.

"Hey, Dick, I've got news for you," I was angry, and I really let it fly. "I've been a head coach. I've got a great job. We go to the Rose Bowl all the time, and most of all, I don't even know if I'm interested in the West Virginia job. If you called me here and want me to create a trail for a bunch of newspaper guys to get screwed up, I'm not your guy. I've got a lot of work to do at Michigan. We're going to the Gator Bowl, and I've got recruits to see in northeastern Ohio, in Arizona, and in Kentucky. I don't have time to come here for this."

Martin knew I was upset, and had a right to be, but he wasn't deterred. He said, "Hey, Don, I guarantee you if I wasn't interested in you, I wouldn't be talking to you. I have talked to both of those guys, but today, I'm talking to you. Nothing is close to decided."

That calmed me down a little, and I told him that Bill and Rey were both friends of mine. He couldn't go wrong in hiring either one of them. Martin told me that he understood that, but nothing was decided. We continued to talk for quite a while after that.

Two days later, the phone rang. It was Dick Martin, and he said he'd like to meet with me again. I was curious. I hadn't written a letter; and I hadn't asked anybody to make a phone call for me. I'd done nothing for this job.

He asked me to meet him at a hotel near the Pittsburgh airport, and that's all he said. I went there at the agreed-upon time and knocked on the hotel door. The door opened and there was Dick Martin and 10 other people.

Another surprise to me—he had never mentioned anything about anybody else being there. I was dressed to go recruiting. I looked okay, but not sensational, which is how I would have looked had I known I was meeting with the whole athletic council. Also, I hadn't brought any materials with me—no resume or other information so the folks on the council could learn more about me or have some information to ask me questions about.

Going into the meeting, I still wasn't sure that I would want the job if they offered it to me. And now I was a little upset with Martin. Naturally, I couldn't tell him that, but I was sure thinking that this guy had set me up. It ended up working to my advantage, another lucky break.

I came across very strong and very confident because I was PO-ed. I told them up front how it was going to be. I told them, "Hey, I coach at Michigan, and we only do it one way there. We do it the right way, and I am not real sure West Virginia is ready to do that. If you're not, then you're wasting my time and your time. If you're not ready to run a program the right way, then find somebody who comes from some place where they don't know how to do it."

I told them straight out, and they listened. There was a moment of quiet, and then Paul Nesselroad from the athletic council said to me, "Don, we want to do it right. Tell us how to do it right."

So I let them have it. I told them how to recruit. I told them about managing practices and how to schedule and how to organize a staff. Everything that I could think of, I told them. I really got fired up. When I left, they thanked me, but I still wondered. I could hear them saying, "Martin, where did you get this clown?" just as easily as "Wow! This guy is sensational." They'd either think I was nuts or they'd love me—there was no in-between.

I left Pittsburgh and went to Kentucky recruiting. I stopped in Louisville to look at a kid at DeSales High. The coach there, Ron

Madrick, was a good friend of mine. We got to visiting and I mentioned that I didn't have a hotel room yet for the night. Ron suggested that I stay in the rectory at the school. It had a couple of guest rooms and it wouldn't cost me anything. I thought that it sounded like a good idea.

We went out to dinner and I got back to the rectory about 8:30 at night. Nobody was around except for the priests who lived there. I went to my room and was just settling in when I heard a knock on the door. I opened it and the father said, "Are you Don Nehlen? You're wanted on the phone."

I was a little spooked that he knew my name. I was wondering how in the world anybody would even know I was there; I hadn't even called Merry Ann to tell her where I was staying.

I shook my head and followed the priest to the phone. It was Dick Martin; how he tracked me down was positively amazing. He said, "Don, after you left, my athletic council said, 'He's it.' They don't want to talk to anybody else. They want me to offer you the job." I was in shock.

He spelled out the deal: they would offer me a salary of $44,000, and I would have a radio and television show that would make another $10,000. By the time everything came together, the package would be close to $60,000.

When I was finally able to speak, I said, "Dick, money is not really the thing that I'm concerned about. I don't want to tell you yes or no right now, because I haven't fully discussed it with Merry Ann."

Mac and I hadn't talked much about it, because there had only been the two conversations and I had been out recruiting. Plus, I knew a move would upset Vicky and Danny big time. I had pulled them out of Bowling Green, a place we'd lived for 10 years, when we left for Michigan three years earlier. Vicky had just started to talk to me again. And now she was in her senior year of high school and in love. She would not be happy about another move. But

Merry Ann reminded me that she was graduating in the spring and was frequently in love with someone new.

Merry Ann and I had never even been on the West Virginia campus, but after talking it through, I decided to take the job. On December 10, 1979, we began one of the biggest moves of our lives.

2

FACILITY IMPROVEMENTS

FUNDRAISING WITH THE GOVERNOR

I came to West Virginia University just as the new stadium was being constructed, but it didn't take long for me to realize what a necessity the new stadium was to building a successful football program.

I was introduced in Morgantown during halftime at a basketball game. During the game, I sat at the press table with Governor Jay Rockefeller. As we were talking, he said to me, "Don, what is your biggest problem in getting this program going?"

I answered him honestly, "Governor, I don't even know yet. But Dick Martin mentioned to me that the site preparation for the stadium has run over by a million dollars. There's a chance they're not going to be able to build any locker rooms or offices or anything else right away. They might only build the stands for right now, and bring in some office trailers temporarily."

(With shovels) Gov. Jay Rockefeller, Dick Martin, and Frank Cignetti at the new Mountaineer Field ground-breaking ceremony in 1979.

I started to get riled up. "Hey," I said, "Jay, with the image of West Virginia right now, all I need is trailers! If we're going to have to recruit out of trailers, maybe I'd just better go back to Michigan."

The governor asked me how much we would need to finish the stadium completely. I did some quick figuring and said about a million dollars. He then asked, "Would you like to come to the mansion and have a dinner with me and some boosters of the University?"

I said, "Sure, I'd be glad to." And the governor replied, "Well, we're going to get you a million dollars."

I went to the Governor's Mansion in Charleston. It was a pretty swanky evening for a guy from Canton, Ohio. After we finished dinner, the governor said, "Men, I brought you here not to feed you, even though I have, but we've got a new football coach, and I like him.

"We've been a doormat, and I'm tired of losing. We think this guy can get the job done, but he can't get it done in trailers. When we complete this stadium, we have to have offices for the coaches and lockers for the kids and a weight room and a training room, and so on—whatever goes with a good program."

The governor said, "Just to show you what I think of this program, I'm going to start this out. I'm writing a personal check for $125,000 for Coach Nehlen and the new stadium.

"Now for the rest of you guys," the governor continued, as somebody else passed out 3x5 cards. "Write down what you think you can give. When we're up to a million, you can go home. If we don't get a million, nobody leaves."

So they passed out the cards and all the guys wrote something down. I was sitting with Orville Thomas, and he wrote down what I thought was $80,000. To me, $80,000 was unbelievable.

When a guy came around and picked up the cards, Orville put his in his coat pocket. The guy collecting the cards left the room to add them up. After a few minutes, he came back in and said, "We're close, but we have to up it some." So they passed the cards around again.

I'm thinking, *Gosh dang it, if this guy would have turned his card in, we'd have had enough.* This time Orville pulled the card out of his pocket and handed it in. When the guy came back this time, he announced, "Governor, we've got it. It's just over a million."

Orville leaned over, hit me and said, "I got you $80,000 extra, didn't I?"

If we had settled for the stadium without the coaching facilities, it would have probably been another 10 years before we got it done. Fortunately, because of Governor Jay Rockefeller, we got it right away. He was the one who went to bat for it. I hope he knows how much his support was appreciated, as well as how much he has meant to the success of the program.

MORE ROOM FOR THE MOUNTAINEERS

After several years of growing success, there was talk about expanding the stadium. As we started to discuss it, Fred Schaus, the former athletic director, was cautious, because it naturally was going to cost a good bit of money. Fred would gladly give you $10 out of his own pocket, but he wasn't nearly as quick to spend the university's money.

If we were going to expand the stadium, which originally sat 50,000, I wanted to add to some of the football facilities as well. When I first came to WVU, our training table and study hall were at the Towers dormitory. We'd lose 15-20 guys going from the stadium to the Towers. We needed to have more space so our team could be together as a group. The WVU president at that time, Gordon Gee, was really great in his support.

Dr. Gee said, "Don, we're hot and we're filling the stadium. If we keep winning, we won't be able to fit them all in." He also understood my concerns about increasing the team spaces. He told me to get an architect and show him what could be done.

Beginning construction on new Mountaineer Field.

Several of us talked with the architect, Fred Krenson. My first thought was to build up, to make the facility three stories high. Krenson laughed and said, "You don't want to do that. Tell me what you need in this addition and let me go to work on it."

When we next met, Krenson put three big outline drawings sketched in pencil on some easels in front of Fred Schaus, Craig Walker (the assistant AD of finance), and me. He said, "What I think we should do is to take this building and push it forward, toward the field. We'll give you basically the same stuff you have in here and give you lots more space in between by taking the new stands in the stadium and wrapping them over the top."

When Krenson showed us his plans, I knew that that was it. He said we would move the banquet room out toward the field, put the weight room underneath, and connect it all with glass so you could look down to the weight room or out onto the field. We were able to have space for a study center and computers, a kitchen, more meeting rooms, and additional space. Plus, I had always wanted to be able to run out onto the field from the locker room, and this plan would make that happen.

The project cost $12 million, and we paid for it, the whole addition. When we finished that, we had one of the most functional football facilities in the country in a single location. It was all here.

The building and the new bowl to the stadium overhead were terrific. We didn't have the money to put the finishing touches and accents on the décor, or the luxury of hiring a decorator (Mike Kerin, our equipment manager, and I hung the pictures), but from a functional standpoint, it was dynamite. Since I've left, Mike Puskar's generous gift has enabled them to do all the decorating. To honor him, the name of the Facilities Building was changed to the Puskar Center.

Another important addition to our football complex was a grass practice field, just across the parking lot from the Facilities Building. It wasn't part of the original stadium plan because of money issues, but too many kids were getting hurt practicing on the astroturf in the stadium. We had more injury problems than you could shake a stick at, especially with ankles and knees. It was just too much wear and tear on our team. We desperately needed a grass practice field, and it would be a great help to us preparing for games at stadiums with natural grass fields. It was Eddie Pastilong, then assistant AD, who found a way to get it done.

Eddie convinced some of our coal donors like John Hardesty, and some of the franchise owers from 84 Lumber to help put the field together. They came in with their bulldozers and graders and built that practice field for us.

Once the ground was leveled, the team would line up every day at practice—all 120 kids and the coaches. We would stand about three feet apart and walk in a line across the practice field, picking up rocks and throwing them over the fence or over the hill. Then we'd turn around and walk back and pick up more stones and throw them over. That was how we cleared the stones from the field.

The original field was about 120-130 yards, and about five years later, we extended it, put some film towers up, and later, we added some lights. The grass practice field was a great asset to our program that is still used today.

The indoor practice facility was something I had felt we needed for a number of years. In the end, Governor Gaston Caperton really helped me get that done. He got us the first million dollars for that building before he left office.

During preparation for all of our bowl games, we were at the mercy of the weather. The worst bowl game we ever played was against Florida in the Sugar Bowl. That December, we ran into 10- and 15-degree weather, and five to six inches of snow at a time. We were practicing in our weight room, running plays for five yards. We had to have the defense practice at three o'clock, and the offense would come in at 5. We'd go out on the game field and practice for 20 minutes and we'd come back in practically frozen. People looked negatively at our bowl record, which they should have, but I thought we'd be much more competitive when we got an indoor building. The indoor building was also a great help when it rained during spring practice and as a place to work out in winter conditioning.

In the mid-'80s, we got some lights installed in the stadium, which gave us the chance to have night games. Night games were something special for Mountaineer football. Every time we had a night game at Mountaineer Field, it was always a big-name opponent, usually highly ranked, and there was national television. Those opportunities turned out great for us. I honestly don't think we ever played a bad game at night.

As far as college football facilities go, West Virginia has got the whole package. We're the crown jewel of the Big East. There's nothing like having the stadium right on campus, with the practice areas right next to it. Our complex has a training table, a study area, computers, a banquet room, a rec room, and every coach has his own office and teaching station. I've had the chance to visit a lot of places, and our facilities are something to be proud of. Nobody has a more functional setup than we do.

THE GREAT LEADERS

All these facilities and improvements wouldn't have happened without great interest and support from the administration, and I was fortunate to work for presidents who were supportive. When I first arrived here, Gene Budig was the president. He was very involved as the stadium was being built. He was interested in athletics and knew that some success in it would make his job as president a whole lot easier. Unfortunately, Dr. Budig didn't stay long enough for us to build a long-term relationship; he left to become chancellor at Kansas.

When Dr. Budig left, Dr. Gee said, "Don, I'd really like to be the president. If you could help with Governor Rockefeller, I would appreciate it." Of course, I didn't have any official influence, but I told him I could certainly let the governor know that I supported him for the promotion. Most people thought Dr. Gee might be anti-athletics, but he was just the opposite. He told me, "Don, I

Ed Pastilong, a former WVU quarterback, became athletic director in 1989.

don't like to tell you this, but this is the first football game I've been to. I'm a Mormon and I've never been very into football, but I like you and your team." I found Gordon to be a bundle of energy and of enthusiasm. Being around him was contagious; he got people excited. He was extremely involved in getting many of our facilities built.

I worked for three athletic directors, and they were all very interested in football. Dick Martin wasn't at WVU for very long after he had hired me, but he was a football guy through and through. Fred Schaus was nationally known, and although his career had been in basketball, he was highly respected as an administrator and as a first-class gentleman to everyone in athletics. He brought a great deal of prestige to West Virginia University just by having his name as the head of our department.

When Fred retired, Eddie Pastilong was promoted to athletic director. Eddie was a former Mountaineer quarterback and very well known around our state. He naturally has gold and blue in his blood.

All of these men were instrumental in my success as a coach and to our program's continued success throughout my tenure.

3

GETTING STARTED

FINAL BUSINESS

When I was offered the WVU job, I said, "I want you to know I will not leave Bo Schembechler's coaching staff until after the Gator Bowl. That wouldn't be fair to him, and there's nothing I can be doing for recruiting over the holiday period anyway."

At that particular bowl game, Michigan played North Carolina, and it was the only time as an assistant coach that I ever went after our team at halftime. The score was close (9-7), but we were getting whipped all over the field. I'd never opened my mouth, but I went after their tails. I said, "You turkeys, I'd like to punch you all right in the mouth. You've got the greatest guy in the world sitting in there and everyone says he can't win a big game, then you guys come down here and lay an egg."

My first year at WVU.

The second half we knocked the crap out of them, but it was too little too late, and we lost 17-15. After that game, I was officially the West Virginia head football coach.

SIZING UP THE CHALLENGE

I took the West Virginia job without much prior first-hand knowledge of what the particulars were, so I did a little investigating. As soon as I had talked with Dick Martin, I gave Gary Tranquill, a member of the Mountaineer coaching staff, a call. Gary had coached me at Bowling Green so I had an awful lot of respect for him as a coach and as a level-headed guy. I knew whatever Gary told me I could take to the bank.

Gary got right to the point with me. He said, "I don't think there are a lot of great players, but there are five or six pretty good ones, and there's a lot of other guys who will work at it. You may really struggle here for the first year or two, but with the new stadium and a little bit of patience, I think that you have a chance."

FINDING THE RIGHT PEOPLE

When I was putting the WVU staff together, I got millions of phone calls from guys all over saying, "I'm this and I'm that." I'm sure there were some good coaches, but I wanted to hire guys whom I knew and I could trust. I came up under Doyt Perry and Bo Schembechler, and they were all about commitment, loyalty, and honesty, so naturally I found all of those things to be very important. Plus, the salaries at WVU were so low, around $20,000 for the assistants; I wanted someone who I knew wouldn't leave for the first higher offer that he received.

Donnie Young and me in 1980—stylish!

Russ Jacques, Bobby Simmons, Carl Battershell, and Mike Jacobs had all been with me before and agreed to come to WVU. I hired Dennis Brown to be the defensive coordinator and kept Gary Tranquill for the offensive coordinator.

Gary Tranquill wanted me to keep Donnie Young on staff, and thank heavens that I did! I didn't have any position filled except for recruiting coordinator. I said to Donnie, "I don't have time to hire a recruiting coordinator, but the thing is, I don't know you. That's not personal. You can try out the position through signing day, and if I feel comfortable with you, you've got the job."

Toward the end of recruiting, Donnie and I were driving back from Beckley, West Virginia, to Charleston. We were winding through the mountains in weather that was half snow, half rain. We could hardly go 15 miles per hour because the visibility was so poor. All of a sudden Donnie said to me, "Hey, Coach, am I going to have a job after next month?"

I said, "Donnie, you have a job as long as I do. But the way things are going here tonight, that might not be very long!" We ended up making it to Charleston safely, and Donnie became a lifelong friend.

THE MOTLEY FOOTBALL CREW

Putting together a staff was an experience, but it was nothing compared to getting acquainted with my football team. When I first walked into the room, all of the players were slouched over looking like a real motley crew. There wasn't a single kid sitting there who had ever played on a winning team at West Virginia. While I was talking, most of them just sat there hanging their heads; they couldn't even look me in the eyes.

Gary Tranquill was the first assistant coach I hired at West Virginia.

I was really disappointed after that meeting. I thought, "Oh, brother, I can see why this team's been struggling." Once I started to get to know the players individually, my opinion really changed.

There was also the issue of getting the players into shape. We were trying to play with 6-foot-2, 230-lb. guards and 6-foot-3, 250-lb. tackles while Pitt and Penn State were playing with 6-foot-5, 280-lb. guys. Of course, there were some players who left. It's not that I told any of them to leave, but some of those guys were better off at smaller schools, where they would have a better chance to play.

That first spring, all I focused on was improvement. I kept telling my players, "We're better than that." I rehearsed with my coaches on how to talk to them; when they criticized the guys in practice, they needed to immediately bring them back up. I wanted the coaches to tell the team, "We can win and we're going to win."

I basically told the team, "I don't know how good we can be, but we can be the best disciplined football team and the best conditioned football team in America, regardless if you're worth a crap, so we're going to accomplish those two things.

"You're going to do what I say, when I say it, and you're going to be strong and you're going to be in condition. We can handle that. Now can you run off tackle? We'll see."

I told our strength coach, Dave Van Halanger, "Dave, these guys better have York Barbell written on their forehead before the season starts." The guys needed to see improvement in something, and I was going to start with their strength. We instituted a very difficult weight training and discipline program, took the neck, chest, bicep, waist, and thigh measurements of each player every couple of weeks. The guys could see their progress inch by inch. They started to believe in what the coaches were telling them and began working harder. By the time football training camp started in August, we wee twice as strong, and I thought that we had a team.

4

COACHING STAFF

IN SEARCH OF
THE PERFECT STAFF

When a football team has more than 100 players, it's obvious that assistant coaches have an awful lot to do with the head coach's success or failure. Any head coach who tries to coach all 100 kids can't coach anybody.

When I was hiring my coaching staff, a few things were really important to me. Number one, I wanted to hire a good person. I was sending guys out on the road on a Sunday night, and they were gone the whole week with my money, representing West Virginia University and the community. If I hired some guy who didn't fit our mold, I'd eventually have a major problem. I was fortunate that the guys I hired were honest, dependable, reliable, and accountable for what they taught on the field.

I used to tell my coaches, "Hey, if that kid makes a lot of mistakes, I'm not going to be on him, I'm going to be on you, because apparently you're not getting the message across."

My philosophy was that I would always coach the coaching staff, but I would never criticize any of my coaches publicly or in front of the players. I would wait until the staff meeting to speak to the offender. I'd say, "In practice tomorrow you change that, but tell them that we were watching the film and saw something that we needed to improve on." We didn't phrase it as something was wrong, rather that we were going to make an improvement.

THE WIVES

I didn't like to hire a guy I didn't know, and I never hired a guy before I met his wife. Wives were very important to me. I used to tell them, "I want you to know what kind of job I'm offering your husband. On Mondays, we meet at 7 a.m. and he's going to get home at 10 p.m. On Tuesdays, he's going to be at work about 7 a.m. and he going to get home about 9 p.m. On Wednesdays, he's going to be at work at 7 a.m. and get home at 9 p.m. On Thursdays, he's at work by 7 a.m., but he will be home by 7 p.m.

"On Fridays, he doesn't have to come in until 10 a.m., and the rest of the day depends on if we're playing at home or away. Sunday is going to be the toughest day. He's going to have to work out his schedule if he wants to go to church Saturday night or some time Sunday, but he has to have his films graded by noon on Sunday. And when the season's over, he goes recruiting."

I made sure the wives knew that as soon as the season started, they shouldn't make plans to do anything out of town with their husbands, because I didn't want them to get disappointed. We didn't punch time cards, but we had to get things done.

At one of my first high school jobs, I was an assistant, and another assistant who was a very, very good coach was run completely out of football after a year because his wife just couldn't hack it. There were a couple of great coaches from Bowling Green who had to leave because of their wives. That taught me early that I couldn't hire anybody until I got a commitment from the wife, because she was part of the team; she had to understand that her husband was going to spend a lot of time on this job.

I'm blessed to have Merry Ann, because she is unique and the best wife a coach could have. When we got married, she knew that I wanted to coach, and she was supportive. She was also unpretentious. Merry Ann enjoyed knowing the other wives and she included them in whatever she could. She would never have a clique, even if she did prefer some of the wives more than others. She thought it was important to include everyone.

When we came to West Virginia, we were a little older than most of our coaches, so those younger women took to Merry Ann. She has made a lot of friends among coaches' wives here and throughout football. A lot of them really looked up to Merry Ann.

It's not an easy role, being the wife of a coach. I think Rita Rodriguez does a good job with it. When Rich was a volunteer coach with us and they were first married, Rita was part of the team that put in the university phone system, and I have liked her ever since. She really works at being a good head coach's wife; people outside athletics don't realize how difficult that is.

ASSEMBLING A STAFF

The first coach I hired at West Virginia was Gary Tranquill. He was already on staff at the university, so I told him, "You can have your choice, offense or defense." He chose offense.

I liked the Michigan defense, so I made Dennis Brown the next hire. In addition, I hired a bunch of guys who had been with me at Bowling Green: Russ Jacques, Bobby Simmons, Carl Battershell,

My first coaching staff at WVU: (from left) me, Dennis Brown, Bob Sutton, Carl Battershell, Bob Simmons, Donnie Young, Mike Jacobs, graduate assistant Bill Kirelawich, Lloyd Carr, Russ Jacques, graduate assistant John Holliday, and Gary Tranquill.

Mike Jacobs. I hired Lloyd Carr from Illinois to be my secondary coach.

We had just started recruiting when Lloyd left for Michigan. I knew that I had to make changes on staff accordingly. Bill Kirelawich had been at West Virginia as a graduate assistant for Frank Cignetti. I was impressed with his intensity. When I walked by, most grad assistants got nervous, but Bill never got nervous. He didn't even see me. He was always extremely focused on working with the kids. I hired Bill for the fire that I knew he could bring to the program.

I knew I needed a recruiting coordinator, but I didn't have time to hire one. Gary Tranquill said Donnie Young, who was Frank Cignetti's assistant head coach, would really like to stay here. I told Gary, I don't know Donnie, because I didn't, and I didn't have much time then to get to know him. What if I hired him for three months and made a decision? Donnie and I talked and agreed to try it until we finished recruiting.

STABILITY EQUALS SUCCESS

One of the reasons West Virginia was so successful in the long run was that we did not have a large turnover on the coaching staff. Of course, some of the coaches were offered great opportunities at other places, but it wasn't like I had three or four people leaving every year. In addition, of the entire 21 years that I was head coach at WVU, I only had to let two coaches go. That track record of stability is unusual for college football. The guys I brought in stayed with me for a long time; many of them were around for ten years or more. The incredible thing about the longevity of our coaching staff is that we were the lowest-paid coaching staff in the Big East with our level of experience I was lucky that many of the coaches stayed for as long as they did.

Of my original staff, Carl Battershell and Gary Tranquill both left after three years; Carl went to Arizona State, and Gary to Navy as their head coach. Steve Dunlap, a grad assistant, left with Gary Tranquill to go to Navy. However, Steve returned to WVU when a job opened here and he eventually become our defensive coordinator. He was the main reason we were ranked No. 1 in the nation in 1996. Billy McConnell left after four years for a position in the pros. Dennis Brown stayed at WVU for eight years before going to Arizona State. Bob Simmons also left after eight years for a position in Colorado. Mike Jacobs left for Ohio State after 15 years. Of course, Bill Kirelawich has remained a West Virginia guy all that time and is still coaching on Rich's staff.

Doc Holliday was a terrific recruiter for 20 years before he left to be assistant head coach at North Carolina State. Billy Legg, my first recruit at WVU, left only to come back later as the coach of the offensive line (later he became the offensive coordinator). Jerry

Holmes was a talented guy who was in the pros for over a decade before he returned to coach our secondary. David Lockwood, another of my former players, later took charge of the defensive backs. The WVU fans can be proud that they've produced so many good young coaches.

One of my former Bowling Green players, Dave McMichael, was on our staff for 18 years. I was fortunate to work with several guys I'd known before, like Dwight and Mike Wallace, Danny Simrell, Bob Shaw, and Paul Krasula. Dwight is now the analyst on the West Virginia radio broadcasts—he still gets to call the plays without any of the responsibility! Dwight's son-in-law, Frank Kurth, was an excellent receiver coach during my last season. Bill Stewart, who is still on the WVU staff, was coaching our quarterbacks right before I left.

Of course, we added some excellent coaches to the West Virginia family. Kevin Ramsey and Darrell Hazell were high-energy guys. Larry Holton was an experienced coach; and I was lucky to have Desmond Robinson with me in two different stints. All those guys and their families still are very special to us.

SUPPORT STAFF

When I came to West Virginia, the football program was awful. They had just gone through consecutive losing seasons, the facilities were absolutely terrible, and morale was very low.

One of the best things I did was to hire Mike Kerin. Carl Roberts was getting ready to retire, so I needed to find someone to fill his shoes. I checked Mike out on the advice of WVU's athletic trainer, Glen Johnson. Mike came in here a young pup, but he helped us get this program running.

My theory on managers was that every coach should have a manager so that someone can set up all of the drills and take care of anything else that needed to get done. Mike helped me start a

Mike Kerin checking out the equipment.

great student managerial program. We were able to give kids financial aid as they gained seniority. My son Danny even became a student manager when he was at WVU.

After a few years, I needed an administrative assistant to take care of all the little stuff for me as the football program expanded. Mike was my first choice, but that left us without an equipment man. Danny was graduating and Mike said, "Coach, you might want to look at Danny to get my old job. He's really dedicated and he loves this stuff. There aren't many college students who love to wash clothes on Sundays, but Danny's one of them. The only thing is, I don't know if the fact that his last name is Nehlen will hurt him or not."

I said, "Well, if he's a good equipment man, what does that matter? Anyway, with what we pay down there, he might be the only one who wants it!"

Danny did want the position, and it was a real pleasure to be able to work along with my son.

Garrett Ford worked like crazy in academics for our athletes. We decided to expand the graduate assistant program so that he would have some help. We had some great people work through that program as assistants and tutors. Sandy Cole started as a graduate student, but ended up staying full-time. She and Garrett have done a wonderful job getting the players to focus on their academics.

STRENGTH AND TRAINING

The most important guy on a coaching staff today is not a defensive coordinator, not an offensive coordinator; it's the strength coach. The strength coach works with the players more than anybody else. If he constantly harasses the players or drives them crazy, then the team will be full of a bunch of kids with bad attitudes who don't want to lift. A successful strength coach mixes up the workout in order to make it interesting and fresh; he's got to make the guys excited to go lift.

I knew that if WVU was going to start winning, we had to have a great strength program. I was fortunate to have Dave Van Halanger on staff. I told him, "Dave, you've got to understand that I want kids that are strong. They've got to be able to explode. They've got to have thighs and hips and necks and shoulders and backs for football."

Dave and I instituted a very strenuous weight program my first winter here. Even though we had very few weights and a tiny, filthy workout room, we did what we had to in order to make every one of our kids stronger.

When Dave left to join Bobby Bowden at Florida State, I hired Al Johnson, one of Dave's grad assistants. Al became an excellent coach. The current coach, Mike Barwis, is a product of that same tradition.

Strength coach Dave Van Halanger helped get our program headed in the right direction.

Athletic trainers also play an important role. I was fortunate that Glen Johnson was already at WVU when I came. My first year, I couldn't figure out where John Spiker fit in. He held his own clinics and did other work, but he was always committed to the teams. The longer I was here, the more I respected his knowledge and the manner in which he handled the kids. They loved him.

John became my go-to guy. I did the interviewing when we needed new trainers, but I always relied on John's advice. He would get three great guys into my office, and I would pick one of them. That's how I got Greg Ott, Tom Colt, and Dave Kerns. The team also worked a lot with WVU students training to become professional trainers and physical therapists.

The team doctors were exceptional. Herb Warden was our team physician. Later he became a member of the first American open heart surgery team in America. We also had Bob Nugent, a nationally renowned brain surgeon. Doug Bowers and Dave Stoll were recognized for their expertise in orthopedics.

The athletic training and medical program at WVU was outstanding from top to bottom.

We were fortunate to have such excellent care. I knew that when a kid went down, we had staff that knew how to take care of him. That's so very, very important.

OFFICE STAFF

The ladies out front are vital to our program because they keep the coaches straight and they are the first people to deal with the public. Ergia Wright was my secretary. I hired Lori Rice after Ergia retired. Lori turned out to be an absolute gem.

I worked with Delania Bierer for about a year. When she headed over to the MAC office, Lori and Tammy Cavender suggested I talk to Kim Calandrelli. Kimmy was the shyest little thing when she came in, but I just loved her. I have never seen two people get along like Lori and Kim, and what they have done for the program is amazing. Dixie Sisler, Virginia Alexander, and Rose Barko were also wonderful to work with. I was so very fortunate to be surrounded by great people.

THE MEN BEHIND THE CAMERA

The video coordinator position became very important at WVU. When I started coaching, I only had 16 mm film to work from, but then we started getting video and computer equipment. The new technology was great, but it created a whole new list of questions. How do I use it? How do I run it? How do I store all of the information? It got so complex that I had to hire a video coordinator. It's hard to find a video coordinator who knows the technology as well as football. We trained some young graduate assistants, and then we hired Don Poluszek.

Don had been the defensive coordinator at Marshall as well as at Carnegie-Mellon. He understood what I meant when I asked for all the run blitzes or all the third-and-shorts. Some guys knew the technology inside and out, but when I asked for something specific, they'd look at me dumbfounded. Poluszek came to WVU with the football background, and Danny Hott worked with him for many years until he got into coaching full time. A lot of people are involved in the video operation, like Jim Galusky and Jim Montgomery, our cameramen. Those two guys were characters, but they were excellent craftsmen and had dedication.

THE IMPORTANCE OF SPORTS INFORMATION

The sports information folks do an awful lot for the football team. When I coached at Bowling Green, sports information was writing a story after the game and adding up the stats, but that has changed tremendously over the years. Now, with how recruiting works, and how important program visibility is, the Sports Information Director (SID) can make or break a team. If the players never see themselves in the news or they feel misrepresented, that's a problem. So much happens with the media these days that the SIDs work non-stop just to stay on top of it all. Scheduling everything for all of the coaches and players can be a nightmare, but the SIDs always kept me on track.

When I got to WVU, Mike Parsons was the SID, and then Joe Boczek filled his position. However, the SIDs who did the most for the football program were Shelly Poe and her right-hand man, Mike Fragale. Shelly and Mike were always so good with the players; they had a way of making everyone feel special. Even if a kid was a lousy player, they always came up with something to involve him or give him something that he could show the folks back at home. I know that a lot of our graduated players still keep in touch with Shelly and Mike.

CAMPUS SUPPORT

Great athletic directors and an interested president are crucial to building a first-rate program. I was fortunate to have some good guys in those positions at West Virginia. We also had tremendous support from the cheerleaders, marching band, and the entire campus. Everybody wanted the football team to do well, and that support made us feel good.

My theory about how to treat the entire staff was simple: everyone needed to feel important in order to have a general high morale. I always went out of my way to make the cooks, the janitors, everyone, feel like a part of the football team. It was important to me that everyone was treated with respect.

It takes an awful lot of people to run a football program. Everybody thinks of the head coach and the assistant coaches, but there are so many people involved. Every auxiliary position is very important in keeping a good solid program, and for the most part, we had people who really cared. West Virginia is very fortunate, from the very top to the very bottom, to have excellent people making things work. Our facilities and reputation place WVU in the top 30 outstanding sports programs throughout America.

5

RECRUITING

THREE RULES
FOR RECRUITING

In college football, there's nothing more important than recruiting, especially when you're trying to establish a program. Every head coach has his own philosophies about recruiting; mine were fairly simple ones.

1. I wanted a young man who would be a good fit for our program. A potential recruit had to have character and share the priorities that we were going to stress while he played for us. Mostly, this meant that a kid put his education before football. In my opinion, the guys who were thinking only of football had it backward.

I always made sure to talk to a recruit first about academics. I'd know what the young man supposedly wanted to study, so that I'd be able to go over the classes and curriculum year by year with him. I'd make sure that he knew how many Rhodes Scholars West

Virginia had produced, and lots of other things about our academic reputation that he probably wasn't aware of. We'd talk about where he was going to live and who his roommate was going to be. I'd tell him about the social life on our campus and was sure to stress the low crime rate in Morgantown, West Virginia. That always impressed the parents. After I went through all that, I would get into the football part of it. I'd detail where the kid would play, how he would fit with our team, why we wanted him. We'd cover what the grant-in-aid included, how long it was for, and how he could lose it. In later years, we would show them some video presentations about the campus and our facilities. We tried to cover the whole gamut.

2. Each year, I had 18-24 grants-in-aid to offer, but I didn't like to even mention it to the prospect until I had met his mom and dad. I wanted to see what kind of family a kid came from and how he acted with his parents. Where the kid's parents lived was also an issue. In my experience, the closer to Morgantown they were, the better. I had found that sometimes when a guy got too far from home, he had troubles. My comfort zone was about a 250-mile radius from Morgantown, although we also looked in Florida for three or four kids a year.

3. I also had a rule for home visits—I'd schedule one hour for every visit. After that, I'd always start to feel like I was infringing on their time or repeating myself. However, I never went in a home where the young man said, "Don't give me the speech. I'll sign," but I went into a lot of homes where the kid had already committed to us, but had started to doubt his decision. For the most part, once we had a commitment from a kid, we didn't lose too many. I would shake his hand and explain that this was a big deal—we were holding a scholarship for him and he had to learn to be as good as his word. Very seldom did we leave a home visit and not know how things would turn out on Signing Day.

Basically, I wanted to make sure that we recruited a kid who had character, was bonded with his family, and wanted a good college education—that was what characterized a Mountaineer type of guy. We relied heavily on the high school coach's opinion of a kid; and the better we knew a coach, the more stock we put into his opinion.

THE SPECIAL WEST VIRGINIA TOUCH

At 90 percent of the other campuses in America, when a prospect visits the campus, the only coach who knows anything about the kid is the one recruiting him. We did something that not many other coaches did. When we had a kid visiting our campus whom we really wanted, I made sure ahead of time each one of my coaches had something personal and intelligent to say.

Our staff would meet and I'd say, "OK, Billy, you understand his dad is an engineer, and Jerry, you understand that the girlfriend is Suzy and she's a knockout, and Darrell, you understand that he's also a great baseball player," and so on. I always thought that personal touch went a long way and was a good recruiting tool.

IN SEARCH OF THE PERFECT PROSPECT

We would send out questionnaires to every high school coach in the state of West Virginia, Virginia, North Carolina, Pennsylvania, New Jersey, Ohio, Maryland, and Florida, asking for their top prospects. Out of about 4,000 questionnaires, we would get back around 1,000. We started the recruiting process with those names.

In the spring of a prospect's junior year, we would start looking at film of the player, as well as talking with the folks at the kid's high school. We wanted to find out as much about the prospect as we possibly could. As a staff, we would make a list of the kids who we thought had a chance to play for us. The guys who made that list were the ones we followed very closely throughout their senior seasons.

We'd make a list of each position, ranking the prospects one through ten. That process was very subjective, and it was easy to make mistakes. Sometime, a guy ranked number ten would turn out to be number one—we were constantly reassessing.

My last five or six years, we started to use a recruiting service. This means that we paid money to have films and reports sent to us. It saved a lot of legwork, because we could make decisions without having to drive all over, but in the end, we were still the ones making the final decision.

There are so many kids out there, that if you're diligent and patient, you'll get your 15-18 kids a year. The key over the long haul is to not make a lot of mistakes. If you get a lot of kids that just can't play at the level of your division, then they're unhappy. Whenever one kid is unhappy, it inevitably spreads to the rest of the team. Eventually, you'll have a locker room full of complainers, because they think that their coach is screwing them and they're not playing. No team is going to win many games with that in the background.

The responsibility belongs to the coaching staff to keep them happy. I used to tell my coaches, "We recruited them. If this guy isn't good enough, it's not his fault, it's our fault. We made a bad decision." Sure, that happens, but if you give out 20 grants, and get 12-13 kids who can really play and the others are good kids who might help somewhere on special teams or as backups, then the program will be OK. If you can bat 60 percent with each recruiting class, you'll have at least 55-60 excellent players on the team, and your program will have a chance.

Recruiting is something I always enjoyed. I never felt it was a hassle. I think if you're going to be successful in recruiting, you have to have that attitude—you have to find something you like about it. If you hate recruiting, it's going to be obvious as soon as you walk through the front door during a home visit. It's kind of like having an English class that you don't want to go to, and you don't like—chances are you aren't going to do very well. If you're going to be a major college football coach, then you know recruiting is a big part of the deal. You've got to get your rump out of the office and go see those kids.

THE FINAL SAY

I had a recruiting coordinator and my nine coaches helping me recruit players. When it came to giving out scholarships, they each had one vote and I had ten—not exactly a democracy. For example, if I had a kid and his family in my office and I thought that he was a good football player, chances were that I would offer him a scholarship, regardless of what some of the coaches had said. It also worked in just the opposite way—if my coaches had wanted to offer a kid a scholarship, if I didn't like him or feel comfortable around him, I wouldn't offer him one.

THE IRRESISTIBLE
DOC HOLLIDAY

A lot of people became impressed with our so-called Florida connection. It started when I went there to speak at a clinic that had an audience of 500 coaches. Afterward, Rick Perry, the head coach at Stranahan High, cornered me. He said, "Don, I'm a West Virginia guy, and I think you're making a mistake not sending a guy full-time to recruit Florida. There are so many great athletes

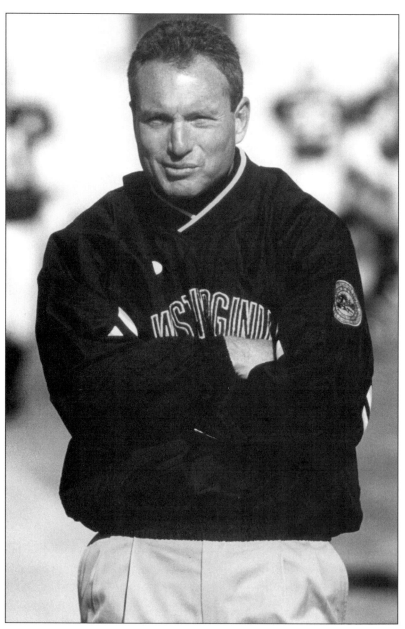

Doc Holliday was a crucial part of WVU's recruiting success.

here, and Florida, Florida State, and Miami just can't take them all. Think it over."

We decided to send Doc Holliday down to Florida. We knew that we had to build a relationship with the coaches to have any chance, so we only picked 50 schools. We figured that if a kid took an interest in us, it would be because he and his coach liked Doc Holliday. Once a guy liked us, we tried to get an official visit out of him. Prospects were only allowed to visit five schools, so we figured if we could get a kid to our school, we'd have a one-in-five chance of getting him to commit. It was a philosophy that just took off, thanks to a great idea from Rick Perry.

Doc never left any stone unturned. He completely surrounded a player. The mother, the brother, the aunt, the sister, the girlfriend all knew who Doc Holliday was, because he took the time to find out who they were and make their acquaintance. I think that in all of the 17 years that Doc and I recruited in Florida, I never went in a house where the mother didn't give him a big hug.

We got Steve Grant, a great linebacker, because of Doc. I thought for sure that Grant was going to end up picking the Hurricanes, but Miami quivered for about an hour, and that's all it took Doc to seal the deal. That was a big catch for darn sure.

Some of my coaches will get mad at me for saying it, but I always thought Doc was one of the best recruiters anywhere. He had to bring kids from warm weather 1,200 miles from home up here in the months of December and January. About half the time, it was ugly, snow and slush, and it was very difficult to get a kid. Doc eventually became one of the most popular recruiters on the east coast of Florida in the Miami-Ft. Lauderdale-West Palm area.

SHINING MOMENTS AT FOOTBALL CAMP

Getting prospects to attend our football camp was a huge help in evaluating potential Mountaineers. Camp allowed us to see the personality, work ethic, and athletic ability that you couldn't see in the films.

Major Harris was one of the kids who stood out at camp. We were recruiting him as a defensive back, but he proved to have speed and was a non-stop competitor. When we played touch-tap football, absolutely no one could get hold of Major. After watching him play, I said, "I guarantee we want this kid." I told him, "Hey, Maj, we want you as a quarterback, not as any daggone defensive back." When he heard that, he was sold.

Rasheed Marshall was the same type of thing. He proved to be such an exceptional person as well as a terrific athlete. I remember watching him jump three feet off of the ground to intercept a pass during a touch-tap game in camp.

RECRUITING BATTLES

Over the years, we won our share of recruiting battles, and those were very satisfying. However, we didn't win many until we started to win on the field, so the very first ones were special.

My first year at West Virginia, I was really excited to get Steve Newberry. Virginia Tech was the only other team recruiting him, but we thought he was the best player in the state of West Virginia, so that was another big win for us.

We went down to the wire with Penn State over Brian Smider. He was a big tackle from Allderdice outside of Pittsburgh. His mom and dad were sold on Penn State, but Dave McMichael had a feeling that Brian really liked us, so we kept on it. We didn't beat

Penn State very often, so when he committed to us, we were very, very excited. Smider went on to be one of the keys to our offensive line on the 1988 team.

Another guy who was really important in establishing our program was Billy Legg. He was the top lineman in West Virginia and a good student who was being recruited by North and South Carolina, North Carolina State, and those teams down in the ACC. We had to prove ourselves to him, so getting him was big. Legg later came back to West Virginia to be my offensive coordinator.

We battled Alabama for big John Ray. They flew their fancy jet in there to make their visit, and I pulled up in my Chrysler. Even though Auburn flew up in their jet to try to get Mike Compton, he chose us because his mom liked us. Aaron Beasley was a kid we really wanted, and Syracuse was putting the squeeze on him, so he was a big recruit.

One of our biggest catches was Quincy Wilson out of Weirton. Not only was his dad Otis Wilson, a former Chicago Bear, but Quincy weighed 220 lbs and had already gained 6,000 yards by the time he graduated high school. He was a recruiter's dream. Otis was still living in Chicago and wanted his son to go to Northwestern or Illinois, but Quincy's mother was great. She said, "Hey, wait a minute, you're going to look at West Virginia before you look anywhere else," and he was sold.

SCATTERBUGS AND SKINNY TURKEYS

There were also the guys who really wanted to come to West Virginia, but when I saw them in person, I admit they made me nervous.

One of those was Willie Drewrey. We went to his home and there's this little kid sitting there; he looks like he weighs 135 lbs.

Willie Drewrey turned out to be a heck of a college football player.

and stands about 5-5. I said to Bobby Simmons, the coach recruiting Drewrey, "I loved him on film, but when you see him and those little shoulders..."

Coach Simmons told me, "When he puts the uniform on, he'll be 6-6, 300." He was right. Willie turned out to be one of the best return men we ever had. Every great football team has a scatterbug, and Willie was a good one.

My coaches thought the same thing about Marc Bulger. When he walked in for his visit, they didn't think a skinny turkey like Marc would last in college football. I had met his parents before and knew that his dad was as big as the door. I figured that Marc still had some growing to do, so I stuck with my decision to take him. Another good call.

Rich Braham was quite a find. I saw him play at a basketball game here in Morgantown and was really impressed. We were out of scholarships at that point, but I really liked him. I told my coaches, "I think we're making a mistake. This Braham is big, quick, and he goes in after that basketball like a wild man. Let's make an effort to get him here." He originally came as a walk-on, but within a year he had put on 50 pounds, and wow! He went on to be a dynamite player and then eventually went pro.

Gary Mullen was another little skinny shaver who turned into a whale of a player. In the Hall of Fame Bowl, Mullen must have had almost 200 yards receiving. Blue Mullen went on to a great career in Arena Football and was one of the first players inducted into their Hall of Fame.

Avon Cobourne was another player who made me say, "Oh, brother, what'd we get here?" Avon was highly recruited as a junior and we really wanted him, along with a hundred other schools. When he blew out his knee, everybody but us backed off. We stayed because of Tom Madiera, Avon's high school coach at Holy Cross who also happened to have been a grad assistant for us. He said, "Coach, this kid is dynamite, and the knee is nothing to worry about. He'll get it back." Tom was right.

Kevin White came to us from Arizona. His high school coach was a close friend of Bill Kirelawich's, and the two spoke constantly, however, we just didn't recruit Arizona. Yet Kevin wanted to come so bad, and we couldn't find another quarterback that year, so we invited him for a visit. We ended up loving him, he proved to be a great little quarterback.

I'll admit up front that I was not a heavily recruited athlete. When I was in high school, Bowling Green was the only school to give me a home visit. It was like that for a lot of my players, too.

Tony Becht is a prime example. He was a first-round draft pick and a successful pro now, but no one was interested in him when he graduated from high school. Other guys whom we almost didn't take were Renaldo Turnbull, John Stroia, Kevin Koken, Rick Phillips—the list could go on and on.

Then there were the guys who were walk-ons because no one had recruited them. Rich Braham, John Holifield, and Paul Woodside all came to us like this, and they ended up having a huge impact on our program.

Donnie Young played a big role in helping us spot the underdogs; he had a talent for spotting the gems that no one else had shown interest in. When no one else was interested in a player, it was easy to get shy and start to back off. That's where Donnie was great. He would say, "Hey, Coach, we've got to go with how we think."

6

FIRST SEASONS

TRADEMARK LOOK

There was no official school logo when I came to West Virginia in 1980. I remember this time well, because I'd be watching game film in order to get to know my team, but I wasn't able to tell which team that was. I thought we were gold and blue, but I wasn't so sure after watching those tapes. I kept seeing different uniforms and a lot of stuff on the helmets. I'd finally have to decide, "Well, that's Oliver Luck there at quarterback, so we must be in white."

I had just left Michigan, and everybody knew what Michigan's uniforms were. You would see the Wolverines on the field and know who it was immediately. I wanted recognition like that.

I called Mike Kerin, our equipment manager, into my office and said, "Mike, I'm not a fancy guy, but chances are we're going to be here for a while, so I want to have gold pants and I want to have blue jerseys. For our away uniforms, I want white with blue numbers on the jerseys.

"I want a helmet that's dark blue; I'd like our helmet to really stick out, be distinctive." The helmets West Virginia was wearing then were white, and they had the state outline and then inside that, they wrote "West Virginia." Sitting in the stands, you couldn't tell what was on them.

I said, "Mike, I would like a gold WV of some kind on the side of the helmet. He asked me what I meant—this brand-new equipment man was sure getting a tall order put on him—and I told him to go down and monkey around with those letters and we'd look at some ideas and see.

Mike came back the next day with some ideas roughed out on paper. He had a couple of different ideas, but the one that caught my attention was the W with the V hooked onto it. Mike Kerin is no artist, and neither am I, but you could tell that if it was done up properly and to scale, that W and V idea would be a good-looking logo.

Before we could go any further, I needed to talk to Dick Martin, the athletic director, because I wasn't sure whether or not West Virginia had an official logo. It turns out they didn't, so I said, "Dick, I'd like to have a logo that's distinctive to West Virginia." I explained my reasons why and showed him the hooked WV that Mike had drawn up.

He liked it and showed it to some other folks in the department: Mike Parsons (sports information director), Eddie Pastilong (assistant AD), Garrett Ford (assistant AD of student services/academics), and Craig Walker (assistant AD of finance). Their response was positive. Dick Martin got his brother John, a commercial artist, to draw it up professionally and to scale. He made it look nice.

We put the logo on the football helmets so that people would identify it with Mountaineer football. When we beat Florida and opened the next season with a win against Oklahoma, the new West Virginia logo became highly visible. It was on every truck and every car in West Virginia, on T-shirts, caps, and blankets, everywhere. I knew then that we had successfully created a distinctive look. In later years, our helmet was voted one of the most distinctive and popular in college football several times. The success of our logo has always been a source of pride for me.

BLUE PANTS BLUES

Throughout the years, West Virginia's uniform has been blue jerseys and gold pants at home, white jerseys and gold pants on the road. I'm traditional, so I never gave any thought to changing it until 1995 when some seniors on the team approached me about it. They said, "Coach, we'd really like to try blue pants."

I wasn't into it, but the guys said it would mean a lot to them. I decided to try the blue pants out for a season. We ended up being a lousy team in blue pants, 5-6. I don't actually think that the pants had much to do with it, but that gave me a reason to announce the blue pants were gone. In the end, they became good practice pants.

THE FIRST SCHEDULE

We opened the 1980 season in Morgantown against Cincinnati. That was some day! It was my first game as head coach at West Virginia as well as the grand opening of the new stadium.

Before the game, they had me sitting out on a platform with Governor Rockefeller, John Denver, and President Budig; we just sat there and sat there during the ceremonies while my team was in the locker room getting ready. And that's where I wanted to be, too! I was completely out of my comfort zone. I was nothing but relieved when the game got started.

The view from above on Opening Day at new Mountaineer Field.

Now I know Cincinnati is not a great football program in terms of tradition, but it was a big day for my team, because there were 50,000 people there. That in itself was something. Our kids were used to only 19,000 or 20,000 at their games, and all of a sudden there were 50,000. Wow! And we won the game.

You've got all those dignitaries there, and John Denver's singing and there was just so much hoop-de-doo for that game. When we won that game our kids really felt good about themselves. Yet the locker room was not like I thought it would be; I thought there would be whooping and hollering, but the kids were just subdued.

They didn't know how to react; they literally didn't know what to do after a win. I finally told them, "Hey, gang, holy criminey, we won! You guys are special!" Then we started to sing our song and have some fun.

We went on to win at Colorado State and then lost a close game to Maryland. We beat Richmond and Virginia. But wouldn't you know that just as soon as were started to get a little bit of confidence, we had to go play in Hawaii?

The Hawaii trip would have been fine if it was the last game of the year, but when you have to come home from that and play Pitt, who was No. 2 in the nation, the next Saturday, it was asinine.

When you went to Hawaii in those days, they used all Hawaiian officials; Tom Osborne, former coach of Nebraska, called me and said, "Don, if you're not 30 points better than they are, you'll have no chance. We went over there and were 60 points better and won by seven."

He was right, although we started out in a very competitive game. But daggone Ollie Luck, our quarterback, got hurt, and I remember six or eight big plays of ours were all called back because of penalties. Roger Dietz was in the game at quarterback, and Walter Easley ran in the end zone, but Dietz forgot to hand him the ball. It was one of those games.

The trip itself was fun for the kids and probably brought us together a little bit as a team. If we had played Hawaii on the mainland on a neutral field, we'd have won eight of 10; that's not the way it is over there any more, but back then, you had problems, and losing that game sure didn't help us.

Down the stretch, however, we still had a chance to win some games. We won two of the last three, but the key game was at Rutgers. The Scarlet Knights were a pretty solid team. They were 6-3 and had only lost to Alabama by four points.

I wanted to find an edge to help us win the Rutgers game. I asked Jack Fleming, the West Virginia radio announcer, to make me a tape of what the game's opening series of plays would sound like. I told him we would kick off, and then hold them on two running plays. I was sure that Rutgers would throw the ball on the third down, so I asked Jack to say that West Virginia intercepted it. I wanted to get that scenario stuck in the minds of my players.

I could not believe how real the tape sounded—it made the hair on my arms stand up. The players thought so, too. They went crazy when they heard us swarming to the ball and then intercepting it.

Walter Easley was a powerful runner.

When we kicked off for real at Rutgers, all of the West Virginia players were flying to the ball on the return. Rutgers ran on the first play for a yard gain. They ran again on second down. Then, on the third down, their quarterback went back to pass the football—same as on the tape. I think that about 11 Mountaineers leapt in the air to intercept the football—and they did! The only thing that happened differently from the tape was the player who made the interception. My team went nuts, and we carried that emotion through to the end of the game. We entered the Rutgers stadium as an underdog and left with a 24-15 victory.

That Rutgers win was a big, big football game for us. It gave us six wins for the year, and if you throw out the Hawaii game, that's a winning season. Even though we had lots of injuries, by the end of the year the team had some self-confidence. The kids worked that much harder in the off-season, and it really paid off in the next season.

A SIGN OF GREAT THINGS TO COME

The second game of the 1981 season was a huge turning point for the Mountaineers. We were at Maryland and down 14-10 with less than five minutes to go. At the fourth down, I called for us to punt the football and make something happen as soon as their guy caught it. Well, sure enough, the return man fumbled. We managed to score a few plays later to win 17-14.

That was a key game for us, because the guys had done what the coaches told them, played 110 percent, and won. We had planned to do something and then made it happen. From that point on, we had a team that believed and kept getting better. We started with four straight wins against Virginia, Maryland, Colorado State, and Boston College—three of those were on the road. We had wins

Radio announcer Jack Fleming (center) was the legendary "Voice of the Mountaineers."

against Virginia Tech, Temple, East Carolina, and Rutgers, and a narrow loss at Syracuse. Our 8-3 record got us an invitation to the Peach Bowl to play Florida. That bowl game looked impossible on paper, but it turned out to be one of the great upsets in the history of Mountaineer football.

7

DISAPPOINTMENTS

My career as West Virginia was great, but for as long as I coached, there were bound to be some disappointments.

THE BLOCKED PUNT

Aside from losing the Fiesta Bowl in 1988 and the Sugar Bowl in 1993, no game was more disappointing than our loss in 1996 to Miami.

It was a night game, and the West Virginia home crowd was great. The Mountaineers were playing very well against a really good Miami team. Our defense was sensational; I think we held Miami to around 100 yards total offense, and we were hanging on to a 7-3 lead in the final minute of the game. With 29 seconds to go, we were at the fourth down, and all we had to do was punt the ball in order to make the time run out.

Miami called time out, and I called the West Virginia punt team over. We had the ball on our 30-yard line. I told my guys, "If you've got to tackle them, then tackle them, but make sure no one gets through." It should have been simple enough.

We got set, and my right guard didn't line up quite where he should have, so the line bowed. In our punt formation, everybody up front looked in to the football; they have to see when the ball is snapped. When it's snapped, the players are supposed to retreat and execute blocking techniques. In that game, when the ball was snapped, my entire team moved except for David Saunders—he hadn't seen the ball snapped. Miami's Tremain Mack keyed the football. Mack was as quick as a cat; he came flying through on that end untouched. He got both hands on the ball to block the punt, then a different Miami guy picked it up and tossed it to a third guy who headed for the end zone. I thought it was an illegal lateral, but the refs gave Miami a touchdown, and they beat us 10-7. That was a quick and painful loss, and it hurt from the ground up—all of our fans were devastated.

THE FIGHT

The second most disappointing game, the 1992 game against Syracuse, was entirely different. In 43 years of football, it's the only game that I thought we won three times, but never got credit.

With three and a half minutes remaining in what had been a competitive football game, West Virginia was winning 17-13. We punted the football, and Syracuse started at their own 18. Marvin Graves, Syracuse's quarterback, ran the ball toward their sideline with our DB, Tommy Orr, hot on his heels. When the play was over and both guys were way out of bounds, Graves threw the ball smack at Orr's head.

I was across the field at the time, so I don't really know what happened next. I just saw chaos break out around the Syracuse bench. The rest of the Mountaineers took off to defend Orr. Before I knew it, my whole team was on the Syracuse side. It took the

Tommy Orr (DB from 1990-93) got the short end of the 1992 Syracuse fight.

officials a while to get things calmed down. Once they finally succeeded, the real ruckus started. Three of our best players were thrown out of the game—Mike Collins, Leroy Axem, and Tommy Briggs. The only Syracuse kid who was ejected was a nondescript player who I don't think had even played a second of the game. The Graves kid who had started the free-for-all wasn't punished at all.

Despite all that chaos, our defense held them. They had a fourth down and decided to go for it, when the referees called David Mayfield, defensive back, for pass interference. That was the poorest call that I've ever seen. First of all, the pass was uncatchable, and second of all, Mayfield didn't do anything. Heavens, our entire offense and most of their defense had run out on the field because everyone knew it wasn't pass interference. The official ran in really late and threw the flag, making it first-and-10. Syracuse went on to win the game.

When I watched the film, I could see how badly we had been robbed: before the brawl, one of the Syracuse coaches swung Tommy Orr around by his helmet; and the pass interference call was just a crime. We complained like crazy to the Big East office. The commissioner had been at the game but had left early to beat the traffic, so he was reluctant to take the whole mess on. I have always been disappointed that the Big East office didn't do anything except review the film to death.

The referee of that game, John Soffey, called me on the phone. He was sick about it and said, "Don, we blew it." That gave me a little bit of satisfaction. I always thought Soffey was one of the best officials around, and his phone call was a class act. I know that stuff happens fast on the field, but when the referees don't know what happened, they shouldn't guess. They made mistakes, and it cost us a football game, as well as the rest of the year—it probably kept us from a bowl.

The next year, 1993, Syracuse was picked as a contender to win the national championship. We went up there and just drilled them, 43-0. We were a team on a mission for that game, and it was one of my most satisfying wins.

THE DOOMED PASS PLAY

Another game that I'd like to play again was our 1997 first-ever trip to Notre Dame.

We went up there with a great game plan, and a great horse of a tailback in Amos Zereoue. Amos went absolutely crazy in that game; he had 234 yards. Quarterback Marc Bulger had a great game as well. He managed to keep Notre Dame a little off-balance throughout the entire game. Unfortunately, in the fourth quarter, we made a mistake.

Talking to Marc Bulger (QB from 1997-99) on the sideline.

We had an over-and-under on their corner throwing the ball. Marc had great confidence in his arm, and he tried to stick it in deep. We should have thrown the ball short, because Notre Dame intercepted the daggone pass. That play never should have been called; we should have just run the football, and run the football, and run the football. It was pure stupidity by us.

The Irish broke a long one, and ended up winning 21-14. It was criminal that we had embarrassed Notre Dame for most of the game, and then lost it at the end. We had problems with that exact same pass again the year that I retired. We had Syracuse beat and we were moving the ball down the field. Brad Lewis, quarterback, had gotten hurt, so we were playing Scotty McBrien. We called the same pass, made the same mistake, and Syracuse scored with nine seconds on the clock. I was mad as a hornet that we had made the same mistake again. When I go to bed at night, I still see those two pass plays.

THE BOWLS

I was always disappointed with West Virginia's lack of success in bowl games. In all of our 13 bowl games, except the two for the national championships, I thought that West Virginia played very well with the exception of South Carolina and Missouri.

The 1994 squad was a very average football team—it was a miracle that we were even bowl-eligible. We started the season with a loss to Nebraska in the Kickoff Classic. We were 1-4 by the end of September when our young guys finally started to catch on. We monkeyed around with Eric Boykin and Chad Johnston at quarterback before we finally decided on Chad; that helped settle the team. We were 7-5 at the end of the regular season and were scheduled to play South Carolina in the Carquest Bowl.

I still think that we should have won that game. It was a fairly close game, 24-21, but I don't think that South Carolina was a great football team. I know South Carolina put a drive or two together that West Virginia should have stopped, but we weren't able to get anything going at the end when we had a chance. That game was South Carolina's first-ever bowl win, but I don't like West Virginia going into the record books like that.

I felt 1998 was my most disappointing season. I thought it was an underachieving team—the players had a lot of talent, but I just couldn't pull it out of them. Our season opener against Ohio State had been hyped up all summer. The Buckeyes were ranked No. 1

Chad Johnston (QB from 1994-1996) drops back to pass.

in the preseason, and they should have won the national championship that year, but we played them pretty much nose to nose. If we had gotten the fumble at the start of the second half, it may have been a different game, but we gave up too many big plays. Losing that game let the wind out of our sails. Had we opened up the season with a win, that team probably could have gone undefeated that season.

West Virginia was criticized a lot for bowl losses, but it was justified when we lost to Missouri in the 1998 Insight Bowl in Tucson. Missouri was solid, but not a great team. West Virginia had much more talent. At the start of the game, we went all the way down the field and were lined up to score three when, my golly, Missouri blocked our field goal and ran it down for a touchdown. We were moving the football up and down the field (Marc Bulger passed for almost 430 yards), but so were they.

We lost 34-31. That turned out to be a very, very, very disappointing bowl loss. Our defense had several guys who have gone on to the NFL—Gary Stills, Barrett Green, John Thornton, Jerry Porter, Kevin Landolt, Charles Fisher, Chris Edmonds—but in Tucson, we couldn't stop anybody. That just drove me crazy, especially because Larry Smith and all the Missouri coaches were Bowling Green guys and such good friends of mine.

LOSING TO A GREAT PLAY

The 1999 loss to Virginia Tech was another dagger, because it went right down to the end. Tech came into the game ranked third in the country, and Michael Vick was having a great year. Marc Bulger, on the other hand, had had a tough year. Every time he turned around, he got hurt. He went down in the season opener.

When we finally got him back, he ended up breaking his thumb in his first game. That left us Brad Lewis, who had not played much.

Brad made a couple of great plays against Tech, and guys like Tony Becht, Khori Ivy, and Jerry Porter made some great catches. Little Avon Cobourne was just a freshman then, but he rushed for about 130 yards, which was unheard of against Tech. We got ahead of Tech 20-19, and had those daggone guys in a third-down-and-long with no more than a minute to go in the game.

Tech was on its own 38-yard line. Vick went back to throw, couldn't find anybody, wiggled around and ran down the sideline. He juked a couple of our kids right on the boundary and tiptoed for about ten more yards. It ended up being a 26-yard gain—unbelievable!

On the next play, Tech kicked a long field goal and beat us 22-20. The loss was hard to take, but at least we lost because of a great play. Vick was a great athlete and savvy enough to sneak away for 25 yards, and any time a team can kick a 44-yard field goal in our stadium with 65,000 people screaming at them, they've earned it.

All losses are tough, but those are the ones that stung the most.

8

GREAT GAMES

After spending the whole week preparing for a game, I'd always be nervous about how the team would play, so for me, every win was a big one. However, the games that were big upsets or really exciting finishes definitely stuck out. Those are the games that the fans ask about and the ones that players bring up years later. At West Virginia, we were fortunate to have several games that could be called "one for the ages."

DAVID AND GOLIATH

No one thought that we had a chance against the Florida Gators in the 1981 Peach Bowl. Even though WVU had already won eight games that year, our program still wasn't respected. The so-called "experts" had looked at our schedule and said that the only teams of any substance on it were Pitt, Penn State, and Syracuse, and we had lost against all three. In addition, we didn't have a marquee player and had played an Eastern schedule, which wasn't respected

Tight end Mark Raugh (1979-82) was a dynamite pass catcher.

at that time. I thought we had a real chance in the Peach Bowl, because that 1981 team got better all the time. The players improved each game and had gained a lot of confidence.

When the coaches were sent to a press conference in Atlanta a couple of days before the Peach Bowl, we took our captains, Mark Raugh and Oliver Luck. Part of the way into the conference, it became pretty clear that Florida coach Charley Pell didn't know my name. He kept calling me "Dan Nellen." Pell made this one comment, "This Dan Nellen has done a pretty good job at West Virginia and they're not as bad a football team as people are saying. We're going to have to get after it a little bit." It was no big deal to me, but it was a big deal to Raugh.

When we left the press conference, Raugh was so mad he was spitting his words, "Coach, I'm telling you that SOB will know your name after this game is over. I can't believe he called you Dan Nellen. I can't believe it."

Raugh was such a leader on that team that the whole squad had heard about it in a few hours' time.

When it came to game time at the Peach Bowl, we had a plan. One part of it was to put a little screen pass in for that game; we called it 88 to the right and 99 to the left. We must have hit Mickey Walczak at least four or five times with that pass. Every time Mickey turned it upstream and gained 5-10 yards.

Another part of the plan was to bring Donny Stemple, our strong safety, off the corner. Florida's quarterback was a rollout guy; he would sprint out and do some things that I thought we could take advantage of. We put Donny to the wide side of the field and kept bringing him in, and he kept knocking the crap out of that quarterback. For some reason, Florida did not adjust to that defensive stunt, so we kept doing it. Florida played into our hands, and we had our first big upset.

Other guys who played really well in that game were field goal kicker Paul Woodside, who made four, Oliver Luck, and Keith

Jones. Keith had been playing over Florida's Galloway, who was the leading sacker in college football and a number one draft pick. He didn't let Galloway touch Ollie even once.

The 1981 Peach Bowl win was huge for all of WVU. It was huge for the Mountaineer fans because they had gone so long without anything much to cheer about. It was huge for the football team because it got the rest of the country thinking that West Virginia could play with the big boys. And it was huge for the coaches and me because it was a sign that the football program was on the right track.

BREAKING THE WISHBONE

We opened the 1982 season at Oklahoma. We were sure to be prepared for that game. The Sooners films had scared us; they were very fast and able to execute the wishbone to perfection. Watching them play just made us sick, because it didn't matter who they played, they ran up and down the field on everybody.

I remember meeting with my team in the spring. I told them, "Hey, gang, we've got ourselves one hell of a challenge. We're going out to Oklahoma to play one of the better teams in America that is led by one of the greatest coaches in college football in one of the great college venues.

"I'm letting you guys know right now that I'm going to tell some fibs all summer long, so don't believe anything I say in the newspaper. I'm going to try to set a smokescreen for the folks in Oklahoma.

"Number one, I'm going to say, 'Why are we even going there to play those guys? Four years ago, we lost to them 52-10, and we've still got some guys here who were on that team and they don't even want to make the trip.'

"The second thing I'm going to tell them is that us boys from the cool mountain air will absolutely die in the Oklahoma heat during the fourth quarter. I'll say, 'My team doesn't want to kill that horse that runs around every time Oklahoma scores. West Virginia's got a nice little team, but this is a mismatch. We shouldn't be playing. We're not at a place yet where we can play a Top 10 team on the road in the heat and humidity. They'll kill us.'"

Then I told my team, "Now men, here's the truth. Number one: it's as hot here as it is there in August, so we'll be in such great shape that we'll make our run in the fourth quarter. If we go in at halftime down no more than 10 points, that's when we're going to win the game. All we have to do is find a way to keep it close until halftime."

Of course, some of what I'd told them wasn't really a lie. It really was a physical mismatch; the Sooners' film made them look like monsters. The wishbone was so hard to emulate in practice that I was pretty sure we would get behind until we adjusted to their speed.

Sure enough, when it came to game time, Oklahoma got ahead of us big-time. I kept telling my guys, "For goodness sakes, don't get flustered if these guys jump out on us." Slowly, we managed to climb back into the game. Jeff Hostetler hit Darrell Miller again and again. We put in a couple of little passes off men in motion, nothing fancy, but it seemed to confuse the devil out of Oklahoma. By halftime, we were up 20-14.

Everything I had told our guys was coming to fruition. In the locker room at halftime, they all were taking helmets and beating the lockers. They were yelling, "Coach, we got 'em! We got 'em! We got 'em!"

The noise was unbelievable! They were so wound up I had a hard time talking to them. They were going crazy, and it made me nervous. I said, "Hey, gang, we've got to play another half," but I don't think any of them heard me. We had convinced our guys that we could kill them in the fourth quarter, and they were certain that they were going to win.

In the fourth quarter we were ahead, 34-27. We popped a 45-yard draw play with Curlin Beck; we split their two blitzing linebackers, and Curlin raced on into the secondary and sealed the win.

As good a football team as Oklahoma was, when they got down by 14 points, they couldn't play. They were tied to that wishbone and couldn't throw the football; they were still giving the ball to the fullback with about five minutes to go. The Sooners were lost, and I knew right then that they couldn't score fast enough to beat us.

Jeff Hostetler really introduced himself in that game. At the time, no one knew how good he was, including me. He did a great job of taking charge of the team, and he threw the ball really well in that game—about 320 yards.

The upset over Oklahoma set the stage for the next 20 years of Mountaineer football. That may have been as good a coaching job as we ever did from both a tactical standpoint of knowing what to do, and getting our kids ready to play.

It marked a rebirth of this football program; that win made it so we could recruit. It changed everything: our fans' attitude and the attitude of our student body. All of a sudden we were somebody, and people latched onto that pride. Since that game, we've had a national reputation as one of the top 25 programs in the country.

I remember that on our way back to West Virginia after that win, the state troopers picked us up at the state line. When they escorted us back to Morgantown that night, I was shocked—I've never seen so many people greet a football team in my entire life. There were maybe 10,000 people in the hospital parking lot by the stadium, and it was literally scary—they were rocking the bus. Some of the players even got out and joined in the pandemonium. I'm pretty convinced that to this day, there still might be some parties going on somewhere for that win.

PITTED AGAINST
THE PANTHERS

It was something amazing when we finally beat Pitt in 1983. At the time, Pitt had a premier program in the Top 10—the defense was ranked No. 1 in America, they had played for the national championship, and a lot of players eventually turned pro. West Virginia had played Pitt in the past, so I knew that in 1980 and '81, they were better than Penn State and Oklahoma (both were Top 10 teams). We had our hands full, for daggone sure.

During game time, there were about 11 minutes to go, and West Virginia was losing by four points (21-17). We had 90 yards to cover in order to score. Jeff Hostetler went into the huddle and said, "Hey, gang, strap it up, and let's get it done." That's when we started moving the ball and hitting some big plays. We moved it all the way down to the 6 and had a first-and-goal play.

Our best play was the power off-tackle play, and I knew Pitt would be jamming it in like crazy. I told Jeff, "Put the ball on your hip and keep it." Pat Randolph threw a tremendous block on their corner. We faked the ball to Ron Wolfley, our fullback, and sure enough, the entire Pitt football team went after him. Meanwhile, Jeff still had the football hidden on his hip and he just waltzed six yards into the end zone. Over the years, that play's been described as a bootleg, but it was just an old-fashioned keeper off the belly. We intercepted Pitt twice to finish the game, a 24-21 win.

It's still amazing to think that in just four years, the West Virginia program had caught up to where we could beat Pitt. The Panthers were a real "who's who" of college football, their defense alone had seven or eight NFL players, and they were our bitter rival. It was really satisfying to beat them, as well as gain some respect from them.

BREAKING THE LOSING STREAK

The 1984 game against Penn State proved to be a big win. I honestly didn't think West Virginia had much of a chance; we had a lot of injured football players on both sides of the ball. It was the eighth game of the year, and we were starting a lot of backup guys who just played their hearts out. Rich Rodriguez was one of them who was dynamite; he had an interception early.

For the winning score of that game, we went to an unbalanced line. We ran a sweep; Penn State was down a man and they didn't shift well enough. Kevin White went up to the line and snapped the ball. Pat Randolph went 22 yards to score on the play. Scotty Barrows pulled around the corner and had a great block that made the play possible. Penn State tried to come back, but Freddie Smalls and Larry Holley both had interceptions to seal the win for West Virginia. One of my favorite plays ever was Holley snagging the ball from Penn State at our own 18.

When there was less than a minute left to play, Joe Paterno, the coach of Penn State, came over and shook my hand. Joe and I were good friends, and I remember him telling me, "We can't stop the clock, and we can't stop this crowd, but this game is over. Let's get our teams out of here."

It had been 29 years since West Virginia had beaten Penn State, and people were going crazy. The word "finally" was flashing across the scoreboard. The Oklahoma win had been big, but this one was more satisfying because Penn State was the so-called bully in our own backyard.

SHOOTING DOWN
THE EAGLES

We hosted Boston College at Mountaineer Field in 1984. The Eagles were ranked in the Top 10, but West Virginia had beaten them every year. BC's coach, Jack Bicknell, was one of my best friends. I had talked with Jack on the Friday night before the game, and he had said, "Here we go again, Don." He was laughing, but I knew that he was confident, because he had a very good football team. Doug Flutie was in his senior year playing quarterback at the time, and he was well on his way to winning the Heisman Trophy.

Boston College got ahead 20-6, and most people wouldn't have given a nickel for West Virginia's chances then, but we kept plugging. We chased that Doug Flutie all over the field. We blitzed everyone that we could find. Matt Smith and Freddie Smalls both came up with sacks to shut Flutie out in the second half. In the meantime, we were moving the football. John Gay and Ron Wolfley were tremendous; each of them had a touchdown. West Virginia ended up with the 21-20 win over Boston College. That was a big, big victory.

THE GAME THAT
DEFIED REASON

Any game against Pitt was exciting, but, oh my gosh, that 1994 game was probably the most unusual game in that series by a country mile. That game had absolutely everything: long passes, blocked field goals, interception touchdowns, an intercepted extra point with a score. You name it, and it happened in that game. West Virginia was up by about 25 points or so early on, but Pitt jumped back in it, and it was back and forth from there.

Chad Johnston was proud to be a home-grown Mountaineer.

We went ahead with about a minute and a half left to play. Even though Chad Johnston made an 80-yard touchdown pass to Rahsaan Vanterpool, Pitt still managed to put itself back in the lead. There were maybe 35 seconds left, and we were down to our final plays. Chad got flushed out of the pocket, so he started to run, and the defensive back made a critical error. We have a drill for that: when the quarterback starts to scramble, the deepest guy doesn't stop. Zach Abraham continued on and, my golly, Chad threw the ball on the run. It was a 45-50 yard throw that dropped right into Zach's hands on a dead stride. Zach took it the rest of the way for a touchdown that won West Virginia that football game. The final score of that game was 47-41.

GREAT GAMES FROM UNDEFEATED SEASONS

Our first undefeated season in 1988 had some extra special wins. The two biggest were against our backyard rivals, Pitt and Penn State. We played Pitt up at Pitt Stadium; they were still a top ten team, and we still had people questioning our potential. A.B. Brown, our tailback who had transferred from Pitt, popped a 64-yard draw play for a touchdown right before the half—had he not done that, it would really have been a tough game to win.

The game against Penn State turned out to be a blowout. We did it with a simple play just before half time that went for a big score. When there was only 30 seconds to go in the first half, they punted the football. My coaches and I just wanted to run out the clock so we handed the ball to Undra Johnson. Penn State blew out both linebackers and corners making it possible for him to go 55 yards for a touchdown. That touchdown made the score 41-8 at the half, and it sealed Penn State's doom. We were ahead so far that we just coasted through the last quarter to get out of there. That was one of the most convincing wins in all my years of coaching.

The win over Syracuse was also very big. Our record was 10-0 at the time, and surprisingly, Syracuse was only 8-2. They were a much stronger team than I had expected, but we had the stadium packed that night, and the football gods were with us. We played very well, but it was when Willie Edwards intercepted them in the second half that I knew we had it. The excitement of the fans as we took our victory lap around the field after the game was one of the greatest thrills I've ever had.

The undefeated season in 1993 also had some huge wins. The Miami game in 1993 was the most electrifying atmosphere I've ever seen in our stadium. We had 70,000 people in there, and it was cold as blazes, but no one ever sat down. The football game was a good old-fashioned slugfest. Both teams played great defense and didn't make any mistakes on offense.

The winning score was a run where we popped Robert Walker on an isolation play. Miami had a little linebacker, and we thought if we constantly hit him, eventually we could wear that kid down. By the time we ran the play to the split side, the kid was so tired that our fullback splattered him right in the hole. Robert had the speed to get in the secondary and score.

It was some kind of thrill to beat a team like Miami, and it was exciting for us to win the Big East championship when Miami was by far the overwhelming favorite. It was a very hard-fought, well-played football game by both teams. That night is one of my all-around favorites.

After that, we had to go up to Boston College. We were 10-0 and they were 8-2, but we were in trouble before we even got there, because we had so many people, players and coaches, sick or hurt—I was dehydrated for two days before the game. Vann Washington didn't even dress, and Jake Kelchner tried to gut it out even though he had a bad arm. Darren Studstill bailed us out, and hit two fourth-down plays over the middle to Nate Rine. It was those two huge plays that kept us alive, but only by a whisker.

BC was still in charge 14-9, and they had the ball down to our own 27-yard line when Mike Logan, a freshman then, recovered a fumble with about two minutes to go. Darren hit a couple of big passes to Mike Baker, and then the one nobody has forgotten—the touchdown pass to Eddie Hill.

We had called 81 deep switch, which meant the ball was going to Baker or Hill—whichever one drew single coverage. Darren read it perfectly, and he threw the ball to Eddie in the end zone for a 24-yard score. The next play, he found Jay Kearney for the two-point conversion, and then Logan picked off a 40-yard Hail Mary in the end zone on the last play of the game to save our undefeated season.

Afterward, BC's coach, Tom Coughlin, said to me, "We can't beat you guys. I can't believe we lost this football game."

I said, "Holy criminey, Tom, I can't believe it, either." And every time I think of that game, I have to pinch myself.

9

CREAM OF THE CROP

L ots of fans ask me, "Who was the best you ever had at this or that?" I coached so many great players at West Virginia, with so many different talents, that it's hard to pick. However, fans and former players love to discuss and debate it, so I figure that my two cents wouldn't hurt.

BLOCKERS

Rich Braham was the best blocking offensive lineman by far. He was one of the few players who didn't block the opposing team just once or twice—he chased them all over the field. We have film clips of him making an initial block, and getting right off of that block to make a second block, and then ending up on a safety 15 yards downfield before the play was even over. He was the most tenacious offensive lineman that I had ever coached without a doubt.

No. 78 Rich Braham (OT from 1990-93) was the best blocker I coached at WVU.

The best blocker in the backfield was Ron Wolfley. He was unbelievable—there was no competition. When we played Penn State, Joe Paterno came up to me before the game and said, "Don, that Wolfley kid's a great player. You tell him that I've enjoyed watching him block all week long on your film. He's the best blocking fullback I've ever seen." Ron did not have great technique like Rich Braham, but he would run over the opposing team—he'd literally just sprint through the other guy.

RUNNERS

We had a number of guys who were good runners in a crowd. Avon Cobourne had an awful lot of skill in traffic. Undra Johnson and A.B. Brown were also good. Amos Zereoue was so powerful that he just carried guys with him. However, Adrian Murrell might have been the best. All the other guys could rip through tackles, but Adrian was able to bounce around them more than anyone else could. We had so many good backs at West Virginia that it's hard to narrow it down.

QUARTERBACK

When people ask me who had the best arm, I ask them, "Strongest arm or most accurate?" The most accurate by far was Marc Bulger. He had a quick release and could put the ball wherever it needed to go. The strongest arm was Jeff Hostetler, and then Greg Jones—who was Major's backup—he had a whale of an arm.

RECEIVER

The best hands of any receiver? Oh, boy, we've had some good ones. Shawn Foreman had awfully good hands. David Saunders had great hands as well. Had he not gotten injured, he probably would have had an outstanding career. The knee injury before his senior year set him back a great deal. Reggie Rembert was right up there with those guys; so was Jerry Porter.

I'd have to say that best receiver is a toss-up between Jerry Porter and Shawn Foreman, with Reggie Rembert, David Saunders, and Khori Ivy just one iota behind them. Come to think of it, we had quite a few great receivers.

BIGGEST HITS

The biggest hit I ever saw was West Turner on a kickoff during his freshman year. It was a hit that rocked the entire stadium. Tim Agee also had an awful big hit. He packed a punch for someone his size coming up from the safety position.

PASS RUSHERS

As far as the best pass rushers, there were three really great ones. I know Canute Curtis led the nation in sacks, but I think Renaldo Turnbull was right there with him, and Gary Stills was exceptional. Those three were as good as they come.

Mike Fox was in a more difficult position to rush the passer. While Renaldo and Gary were normally blocked by only one guy, Mike Fox was blocked by two. However, Fox had the best push of any of the four, although he was not near as quick or agile. Gary

Canute Curtis and me at the 1996 Butkus Awards.

Stills was the quickest off the ball, but Renaldo was 6'5" and had the reach to go with it. Canute was a blend of speed and reach, but he played his senior year with tremendous focus.

DEFENSIVE BACKS

With defensive backs, there were a couple of guys whom the opposition always threw away from on purpose. Aaron Beasley was about as good a cover guy as we ever had. He was a terrific athlete and had a knack for getting the ball. Steve Newberry was also an awfully good cover guy. Those two got the job done pretty darn well. Fulton Walker made a great corner, but when he played, they didn't throw the ball that much. Corners were always better cover guys than safeties, but I've got to mention Mike Logan, because he was always at the ball. Mike also wins my vote as our unluckiest player—he had the same arm broken three times. That's a record no one else wanted.

PUNTER AND KICKER

Our best punter was Todd Sauerbrun, and our best field goal kicker was Paul Woodside. Both of them set NCAA records, and both of them had what you would call a "wacky" kicker's personality.

LEAPERS

The best leapers were Renaldo Turnbull and Jerry Porter; Theron Ellis would be just a whisker behind them. Those guys could really get up there, and they made some big plays that changed games.

FASTEST

The fastest guy I coached would have to be our Olympic guy, James Jett. He had tremendous speed. The thing about James Jett that amazed me was that some track guys don't have football speed, but he had it. Even with all of the pads on, he could still run just as fast as he could without them. He could fly whether or not he was carrying the football. All of his years in the pros definitely proved his talent.

Of course, James Jett is the only Olympic gold medalist that we ever had. He ran on the 100-meter relay team in the Barcelona Olympics in 1992. That was before his senior year. It was really something—one week, we were watching him on TV competing in the Olympics, and just a few days later he was back at WVU for training camp. He was a very unassuming guy, but so, so fast.

That question of who is the fastest is easy to answer; however, I'll say one thing—Antonio Brown could have given James Jett a run for his money in the 40-yard dash. The fastest running back I ever had was probably Adrian Murrell, another quality pro.

FEARLESS

I can't pick out just one guy who was the most fearless, because I had a lot of kids who played without any fear. They were tough guys who loved physical, smash-mouth football.

I know that Darryl Talley had no fear. But neither did Mike Fox, Ron Wolfley, Freddie Smalls, Barrett Green, Chris Parker, Bernard Russ, or Rich Braham. There were so many guys who were fearless; I could probably name 30 or 40 more guys. Fearless guys were crucial when it came to the nitty-gritty of winning games.

UNBELIEVABLE PLAY

The most unbelievable play was Major Harris' run against Penn State in 1988. I had called 37 and he ran 36. Everybody else on our offense went one way, and Major went the other—he literally ran through the Penn State defense for a touchdown of about 30 yards. After he had scored, Major came to the sideling and apologized. He said, "My fault, Coach." People still ask me about that play all of the time. Fans and coaches still talk to me about Major Harris like they saw him play yesterday. If there was a contest for most exciting player, Major would win it hands down.

BEST OVERALL

It's not as easy to pick the best overall athlete, because the "combination" kid who played football and basketball went out of vogue. Major Harris was a great athlete—he could have been a great basketball player or have done well in almost any sport. However, Jerry Porter was probably the best. He was great at running, jumping, catching—all those things. I know there are plenty of other guys who were great all-around, but Major and Jerry made most of what they did seem effortless.

10

A-Z

People ask me all the time, "What was so-and-so like?" It would take me forever to cover all the guys that I've ever coached. Someone once added it all up, and there were something like 900 players I coached in all of my years at West Virginia. I am bound to leave plenty of great kids out, but here are a few of the ones I get asked about the most often.

TIM AGEE

We found Tim Agee in a freshman football game. He was a kid that no one really knew about, but his dad was a West Virginia alum, so he wanted to come here. He walked on to our team as a punter even though he had been a quarterback in high school. We were scheduled to play Ohio State in a freshman game, and Steve Dunlap was getting our team ready. Steve said, "Coach, we don't have a free safety. We barely have 22 guys."

I looked over the list and said, "What about Tim Agee? You've got him as a punter."

Steve said, "Yeah, but he's a punter. He's never even lined up back there."

However, we literally didn't have anyone else who could cover the position. Steve put Tim in as free safety and told him not to let anybody run behind him. As soon as the game started—holy jumping catfish—Tim Agee was all over the field, tackling guys at the line of scrimmage. I was in the stands trying to figure out what player was doing all of that. From then on, we always put him at free safety, and he was a real hitter. He had a great nose for the ball and was really smart. Timmy couldn't run 4.5, but he was a solid 4.7 kid, and smart enough to know that in a passing situation, he just backed up a yard. He knew the game of football. People didn't run behind him, and when they caught the ball in front of him, he punished them. He's gone on to a long career as an actor—amazing.

MIKE BAKER

Mike Baker was my kind of player—a guy who just loves to play. He was a dynamite football player, and a big-time receiver—he was just an enthusiastic guy. Mike was one of our better receivers, and he had the personality that could convince all of the other guys that a big play was just around the corner. He had loud, vocal confidence.

AARON BEASLEY

Aaron Beasley was pretty heavily recruited out of Pottstown, Pennsylvania, and thank goodness that we got him. He came to us in the same class as Mike Logan, Charles Emanuel, and Vann Washington—and all four of them went to the NFL. We had to play Beasley as a true freshman, because we needed him and he was so talented. He was a great cover guy, and teams were throwing the ball more by then. His cover skills kept him in the NFL for many years. One thing about Beaz was that he loved to practice. He'd come running out onto the practice field, flying around and having fun. It was really obvious how much he loved the game of football.

ANTHONY BECHT

Anthony Becht was 6 feet, 5 inches, 205 pounds in high school, but very few recruiters even looked at him. We had him in for a visit, and just fell in love with Tony and his family. I really liked him, and I knew our weight coach, Al Johnson, could put 30 or 40 pounds on this guy if he worked at it. That's exactly what happened, and Tony turned out to be a tight end who supplied us with a lot of weapons. After college he went on to be a No. 1 draft pick.

Tony Becht is a perfect example of how people who get so excited about recruiting according to rating and amount of stars are completely missing the boat. Heart and character can't be measured. Tony's character is impeccable—you could trust him with your life.

RICH BRAHAM

Rich Braham was not only the best blocker in all of my time at West Virginia, but also one of the best success stories. He came out of Morgantown's University High recruited by almost nobody. We had already given out all our scholarships for the year, so we talked him into coming into the program as a walk-on. Before the year was out, Rich Braham had earned a scholarship, and we knew we had something special.

Rich Braham accepts his All-America award.

Rich never stopped working on his technique, in the weight room, or in any other way that he thought might make him better. His work ethic was tremendous, and he was a down-to-earth West Virginia guy who got along with everybody. On the field, he was fierce, but otherwise, he's just an easygoing guy who takes it all in stride. I think his demeanor and work ethic are why he's still playing in the pros 15 years later. Rich Braham is as good as they come.

A.B. BROWN

How A.B. Brown came to us is some story. It was a Sunday night in 1985, and the coaches and I were sitting in the staff room getting ready to play Pitt. We were watching film of A.B. Brown running the football when the phone started ringing. We rarely answered the phone on Sunday nights, but one of the grad assistants picked it up. He came into the staff room and said, "Coach, the guy on the phone says he's A.B. Brown, and he'd like to talk to you."

I was thinking that it was probably a practical joke, but I took the phone anyway. The guy said to me, "Coach, my name is A.B. Brown, and I play for Pitt." I knew who he was—I was watching his film right at that moment—so I told him so. A.B. said, "Coach, I want you to take a good look at me when we play on Saturday, because next year, I'd like to transfer to West Virginia. I just want to make sure you want me on your team, so please take a good look at me Saturday."

That Saturday, A.B. gained over 100 yards on us. He was a big-time back, but he just wanted a change. The only thing he lacked was blazing speed, but he was real good from tackle to tackle. I used to kid him because he had bowlegs, but A.B. Brown was a whale of a player. Now he's a tennis pro—that tells you what kind of an athlete he was.

MARC BULGER

Marc Bulger wasn't a big guy in high school, and he hadn't played much football until his senior year. However, when I watched him on film, he was the best pure passer I had ever evaluated. When he came to campus, I only had to watch him throw for about three days before I knew he would be special. Marc had the most natural delivery of any kid I ever saw, and he got rid of the ball very quickly. When he decided to throw the ball, it was flat-out gone—there aren't many guys today in the NFL with a delivery near Marc Bulger's. He learned the offense, he knew what we wanted to do, and he looked like nothing ever bothered him. He still looks like that when I watch him play today. He's like a duck—on the surface everything looks awful smooth, but under the surface, those feet are going 100 miles an hour. Marc Bulger looks like the calmest guy in America, but he's into the game big-time; he knows what's going on, and he lives and dies with it.

TODD CAMPBELL

Todd Campbell, along with Oliver Luck, was probably the best player we had when I got to West Virginia. I had tried to recruit him for Michigan. Maybe he didn't get the ink a lot of guys got, but he was really a force along our defensive line. He gave us an anchor to build around up there. He was a great competitor.

DEREK CHRISTIAN

Derek Christian was a big-time linebacker on some of our early teams. He was really a great player and a lot better than most people ever realized. At the time, we played a 5-2 defense; over those guards he was a handful in there. When we recruited him, a lot of people weren't sure that he would end up with playing time, but he had a great four years. We were just pleased as punch with him.

AVON COBOURNE

The story of Avon Cobourne just shows how some recruiters can really mess up. Everyone was after Avon while he was still in high school, but after he injured his knee during his senior year, a lot of people backed off. We might have as well if it had not been for Tommy Maderia, his head coach. He told me, "Coach, he's a great player and he's doing everything he possibly can to get his knee back." So we took Avon, and all the rest is history.

Avon had great vision—he made the great cuts—and he worked very hard to make himself a great player. He had God-given talent, and he really made the most of it. Avon was as just as productive without the ball as with it. He was a great guy to have on the team.

MIKE COLLINS

Mike Collins was a real headhunter. He was one of those strong safeties who could really smack other players. Mike could flat-out hit someone every time. He was a Huntington kid, and we hadn't had a lot of guys from there, but he took great pride in playing for West Virginia. He was a team-builder, lots of personality and energy, and that made him a great captain for us in 1993.

MIKE COMPTON

Mike Compton was not just an All-American at center, but from a recruiting standpoint, he was the best offensive lineman we ever got. And that time, the so-called experts were right, because he turned out to be a tremendous player. He started with all the intangibles—he was big, strong, mobile, and smart—plus he worked at improving. He did the same thing in the classroom, and that's what kept him in the pros for about a dozen years. Some people underestimated him, because he was a country guy and talked with a twang, but he was as smart as they come, and he knew the game of football to every advantage. He was inducted into our WVU sports hall of fame last year. Usually, it makes me feel old to see one of my players inducted, but I am so proud that a guy like Mike Compton represents West Virginia that I don't care.

CANUTE CURTIS

Big Canute Curtis ended up setting our sack record. He turned out to be a great pass rusher, and his senior year was one of the best seasons any defender has ever had at West Virginia. He was a running back in high school, but he was a natural on defense. His attitude was great and he worked very hard every off-season. He really respected our coaches and blossomed under their attention. Canute had everything going for him: speed, size, and agility. We played him at a position where the opponents more often than not screwed up and didn't block him. That was a bad thing to do with Canute on the field.

ERIC deGROH

Eric deGroh was one of the smartest guys ever to play college football. He was not a highly recruited kid, but he was 6 feet, 4 inches, 240 pounds, and had played Ohio football—I thought that he was worth the gamble. The center does a lot of things that nobody knows about—pass protection and keeping both guards straight—and Eric was smart enough to do it well.

From an academic standpoint, Eric was unbelievable. He went through our place taking the hardest courses in science and math that we had to offer. In the summer, he conducted research experiments over at the hospital. A guy like Eric deGroh will come up with a big discovery some day.

WILLIE DREWREY

When we were recruiting Willie Drewrey, I remember telling Bobby Simmons that I thought it would get us fired, because Willie was so small—probably only 145 pounds soaking wet. However, his film showed him playing like a 200-pounder. He was a great punt returner and a real threat. He made our special teams exciting to watch. Pound for pound, I'd take a lot more Willie Drewreys.

WILLIE EDWARDS

Willie Edwards was a Morgantown guy. When we recruited him out of Morgantown High, everybody thought Tony Johnson would be the big star and Willie would be the hang-on guy. It turned out that Willie was the one who made it as a star. Willie is one of the nicest guys to ever play for the Gold and Blue, and he made one of the biggest plays in the history of West Virginia football. One of the biggest victories in West Virginia history was Syracuse in 1988. Willie picked off a pass in the second half and ran it in for a touchdown. I knew right then we were going to win and have an undefeated season.

SHAWN FOREMAN

Shawn Foreman was one of the most special young guys I ever coached. He had something about him that everybody just loved, and it was contagious. He had big mitts and could catch anything—he had some of the best hands of any receiver we ever had. In addition, Shawn was a tough guy who was not afraid to take a hit—a real football player. He was elected captain his junior and senior years. His positive attitude was infectious.

DENNIS FOWLKES

Dennis Fowlkes, out of Columbus, Ohio, was a young linebacker on my early teams. He was a tremendous player, with a tremendous attitude. He was just fun to coach, and he made the guys playing alongside him enjoy the game more. He had a manner about him that was contagious. I loved coaching a football team with Dennis Fowlkes on it.

MIKE FOX

Mike Fox was a dominator along our defensive line—a real force inside for us. He had a great push, and was so strong that he could block anybody. He was a tough-nosed guy who loved the contact along the trenches. After he got out of pro football, he did very well for himself as a businessman in the Charlotte area.

DAVID GRANT

David Grant was probably the first great defensive lineman that we had, and he played in the NFL several years. David was a tremendous player for us up front—just a tower of strength. He was a dominator along the line. When he got hurt, it really cost us, because our early teams had no depth, let alone somebody who could replace a player of his talent. He's doing great now; he's the strength coach at Seton Hall, another great ambassador for Mountaineer football.

STEVE GRANT

I thought that Steve Grant was amazing. He was about a 175-pound linebacker in high school, but he grew into quite a player. When he came to us, he was sort of lost in figuring out his life, but he got involved with FCA and really took to it. He became a great leader for our football team, and a whale of a player—big and strong. He went on to start for the Colts, and now he's one of the great motivational speakers in the country. He's sensational, and he made himself that way through hard work. I'm awful proud of Steve Grant.

BARRETT GREEN

I'm also proud of Barrett Green. His dad played for me as well, so I know they are both outstanding men. Barrett is a keg of dynamite, an extremely physical football player. We had to do a little work when he came to us because he didn't know when to hit somebody and when to slow up because the opponent was out of bounds. However, we never had to teach Barrett how to hit. He would flat-out nail someone. He could run and he could strike, and do it all with a smile on his face.

CHRIS HAERING

Chris Haering is a guy I never thought would come to West Virginia. Mike Jacobs and I went out to Pueblo, Colorado, to recruit him. All the while, I'm sitting in this kid's house thinking what are we doing out here? He had a great mom and dad, but Colorado and Colorado State were both recruiting him. However, he had family living in Pittsburgh and that really helped in his decision to go to WVU. Pound for pound, Chris Haering was probably the best linebacker we ever had. He was built like me—no legs and no chest—but he started for four years as an inside linebacker. He's done a great job as a high school coach in the Pittsburgh area.

MAJOR HARRIS

Major Harris was the most exciting player we ever had. He made an awful error by leaving early, but he was listening to what his family wanted him to do. He was a great option quarterback, maybe one of the first. A lot of what I see in the game today is stuff that Major excelled at. He was very strong and never got hurt; that's why it was unbelievable that he got hurt the third play of the game

Barrett Green (LB from 1996-99) was every bit the player his dad was.

in the Fiesta Bowl. That's a game where we really wanted to showcase him. I don't want to sound like I'm making excuses, but Major's injury made a huge difference in that game.

Major was exciting as could be, and he was the perfect fit for what we were trying to do. He had a different kind of wit, and he loved to compete in anything—everything was a contest or a game to Major. I was glad when he came back to finish his degree, because Major Harris is one of the really magical names in Mountaineer history.

JEFF HOSTETLER

One of the reasons we were able to keep this program going at the beginning was Jeff Hostetler. Oliver Luck was solid, but we couldn't recruit anybody at quarterback because we had no reputation, no tradition, nothing. When Jeff transferred here from Penn State, he gave us a blue-chip guy waiting in the wings until Ollie graduated. Jeff had it all—brains, size, he could throw the football and run it. All you need to know about him is that he played in the NFL for 15 years, and has a Super Bowl Championship. Jeff was one of the better athletes we ever had. Plus he had an eye for good-looking women, which is proved by the fact that he married my daughter. Jeff's part of the family, so naturally he's very special to me.

BRAD HUNT

Brad Hunt, the Ripley bomber, was a great defensive football lineman until he got hurt. The injury slowed him up physically, but nothing could slow down his enthusiasm. He was gung-ho all the way. Brad was so proud to be a football player from West Virginia and was a great Mountaineer. He still is.

Jeff Hostetler (QB from 1982-83) before he became my favorite son-in-law.

KHORI IVY

Khori Ivy was a very talented receiver. He could catch anything, and he understood the position so well that it was hard to defend him. He had an effortless ease on the field and off of it. Khori Ivy was supposed to go to Tennessee, but they didn't end up taking him—their mistake—because he was a real gem. Khori is a guy who is polite, smart, and a positive influence on everyone around him. He will be a success at whatever he tries. I'm thankful and proud that he was a part of the Mountaineer football program.

UNDRA JOHNSON

Undra Johnson came from a tough situation out of Stranahan High School in Ft. Lauderdale. He was one of the first guys we recruited out of Florida—kind of an icebreaker for us. He turned out to be a lot better football player than I thought he would be. Undra was a tremendous slasher for a tailback—tackle to tackle, he's as good as we ever had. And although he didn't come here with a real strong academic background, he turned out to be a great student. Undra made it because he wanted to, and he's done great ever since. Today, he's a vice president of a financial group. I like to call him up and ask, "How much of my money did you lose today?"

CHAD JOHNSTON

Chad Johnston was our quarterback for three years. When he started out, the battle was between him and Eric Boykin, but Chad gutted it out and got the job. He was everything I could have asked for: a super kid, a super hard worker, and a West Virginia guy who was so proud to be our quarterback. He was gutsy, tough, and had the confidence of the entire team. Now Chad's a medical doctor, so that gives you some idea of the type of focus and character he has.

BRIAN JOZWIAK

Brian Jozwiak is probably as good an offensive lineman as we ever had. He had a sensational junior year, and all the pros were in love with him. He didn't have the great senior year that we expected, but that was due to an injury that we really didn't know about. We thought he had a pulled groin, but it was really a long-term hip problem. That was a real shame, because it cost him a lengthy pro career. Brian was awfully big and strong—really the first great lineman we had under my tenure.

JAKE KELCHNER

Jake Kelchner transferred in from Notre Dame. He was one of those guys that you couldn't help but love. Jake was a winner from the word go. He had a contagious attitude about him. He thought that he could lick the world by himself, and the kids picked up on it. He wasn't all that fast or all that big, but he threw the ball well. He just believed in himself so much and he got it done on his attitude.

KEVIN KOKEN

Kevin Koken was the leader of the 1988 offensive line. That line stuck together and took its lumps as sophomores, but they came together as juniors and had a great year as seniors. Kevin was the catalyst for it all—just a wonderful young guy from Youngstown, Ohio. He had a way of bringing people together. He has gone on to manage several states out West for Federal Express. I spoke at a meeting for his company a few years back, and afterward his boss said to me, "Coach, if you have any more like this guy, we want 'em."

BILL LEGG

Bill Legg was my number one; the first kid I ever recruited to West Virginia. I remember telling Merry Ann, "The best football player in West Virginia plays for the Polka Dots— good luck!" Billy Legg turned out to be a much better player than I thought he would be. He was a three-year starter who dedicated himself to the weight room and became big and strong—an excellent football

Billy Legg (OL from 1981-84) came back to join my staff; now he is the offensive coordinator at Purdue.

player, and as smart as can be. Later on, Billy ended up on our coaching staff for quite a few years. In my opinion, he's as good a coach as there is out there, and he's one of our graduates. Some school better grab him to be a head coach or else they're making a big mistake.

BRAD LEWIS

Brad Lewis was a guy who filled in for us when Marc Bulger got hurt during his senior year. I've got to give Brad a lot of credit, because a lot of people weren't real kind to him. The quarterback position at West Virginia University is so visible, but I thought Brad was very solid. The kids really liked him. He was big, strong, and kept improving. He showed us some of the things he could do in the Music City Bowl that we hadn't taken advantage of earlier. Going into that bowl, I decided to throw caution to the wind because I didn't think we had near as good a football team as Mississippi. We did some different stuff, and Brad executed it about as well as any quarterback we ever had.

DAVE LOCKWOOD

Dave Lockwood was an outstanding corner from the Philadelphia area. He was a cover guy and did a great job. Years later, we brought him back as a coach and now he's the defensive coordinator at Minnesota. He's always had that type of attention to the game—an excellent football guy. Dave is another great ambassador for West Virginia football.

MIKE LOGAN

When we recruited Mike Logan, we thought we got the best player out of Pennsylvania. Unfortunately, he broke the same arm three times. Because of that, it's impossible to know what kind of career he could have had. Even with the injuries, Mike Logan was a dynamite football player. Physically, he was the toughest defensive back we ever had. He could really bring it. I'm glad that he has done so well in the pros.

OLIVER LUCK

Oliver Luck was already at WVU when I got there, thank goodness. If he hadn't been, we'd have been in real trouble. We just had the one quarterback; if Ollie went down, we'd have had to go to the single wing or something. He got us through, and he was the most respected guy on the team. He was a dynamite young guy— the whole package. He's in charge of the Houston sports authority, but he's still just a down-to-earth guy. In my opinion, we need a lot more Oliver Lucks in this country.

RASHEED MARSHALL

Rasheed Marshall is a guy we recruited because he could jump out of the daggone sky. He was very skinny when we recruited him, but in our summer camp he showed me great athletic ability. Rasheed is about as nice a young man as God ever put on this earth. His mother sent him to prep school for a year and then we redshirted him a year to give him time to physically develop. That made him a great player for the future. He and his buddy Quincy Wilson are two of the finest kids we ever recruited.

DARRELL MILLER

I love old Darrell Miller. Darrell was my hop-a-long wide receiver with the bad knee. He had great hands and was tough across the middle. We ran a pattern where he ran a trail about 14 yards deep; when he caught that ball he got nailed every time, but it never bothered him a bit. He was a courageous kid. He was a big receiver with a lot of talent.

GARY MULLEN

What I remember most about Gary Mullen is that great touchdown catch he had in the Bluebonnet Bowl and a pass from Jeff Hostetler against Miami when UM won the national championship after Gary caught the ball in the end zone, but was called out. Blue Mullen was a great player for us and just an easygoing guy. He had great hands, great speed, and he played a million years in the Arena league, going to the AFL Hall of Fame.

ADRIAN MURRELL

Thank goodness some alum wrote me a letter about Adrian Murrell that said, "You ought to check this kid out in Hawaii." We didn't think we had a chance to get a kid from Hawaii, but Adrian wanted to come to the East Coast. It definitely didn't hurt that his dad was in the service and was going to be stationed in North Carolina. Adrian had great acceleration—a great kid to bounce and go around the opposing team. He was very shifty, and probably the fastest guy with the football that we had at tailback. No wonder he was a starter in the NFL for all of those years.

STEVE NEWBERRY

Steve Newberry is Mr. West Virginia as far as I'm concerned. He did a great job playing football for us. I don't think we've ever had a better person than Steve wear the Gold and Blue. He loves this program. There aren't many guys like Steve Newberry, and that's a shame. The good Lord should have patented him and kept producing them, because he's special.

BO ORLANDO

Bo Orlando was a different breed, a cut above. He had played quarterback in high school, but he knew that he would have to play somewhere else in college. Bo was a lot like Tim Agee—he flat-out popped you, and he had good speed. Bo was not only a great football player, but was also an excellent leader for us. Bo Orlando came out of the Berwick, Pennsylvania program, that sent us some terrific players, and he was as tough as nails. Every team needs a Bo Orlando.

WES OURS

Wes Ours? I loved him. He was our little fat fullback. When you coach, there are certain kids you fall in love with because they're so much fun to be around, and Wes was one of those guys. The fans just loved him, too. We moved him to guard, and he was good there, but we kept moving him back and forth. What I remember best was that for the Music City Bowl, we put in a play off the fake reverse, because Mississippi played straight man to man. We faked an isolation play, and the linebacker came up to the hole to make the tackle, and we slipped Wes right by him. The quarterback faked to the tailback, then faked to the wide receiver (the reverse guy), then Brad went back and threw the ball to Wes as he ran down the sideline. Wes just kept going and he scored. It was the play in the Music City Bowl that set everything off. Wes Ours was a gem.

JERRY PORTER

The amazing Jerry Porter was just too good an athlete for his own good. Consequently, we played him in too many places, and that fouled him up. Had I not had Marc Bulger on our team, Jerry Porter might have been West Virginia's quarterback. However, Jerry could also play several other positions that Marc couldn't, so we decided to make Jerry a wide receiver. He was a great receiver. He could catch the ball like crazy; but all of a sudden, we had a ton of injuries in the secondary. We couldn't even line up—we were in deep doo-doo back there. Jerry was a great athlete, so we moved him back there. None of us were happy about it, but we had to put 11 guys on the field. He was an average defensive back, and when we had a chance to move him back to offense, we did. Jerry was always a colorful character, a real cut-up. He had energy in everything he did. And Jerry's been a great pro, a really talented kid.

MARK RAUGH

Mark Raugh was by far the best tight end we ever had. He weighed about 215 pounds, could catch anything, and blocked like crazy. He was a real football player, a highly competitive guy. He brought that competitiveness to the field every day. When I got this job, he was one of the players who made it special.

JOHN RAY

John Ray could have been the best offensive lineman we ever had here. He had the speed and power—he had everything that it takes to be a superstar. Unfortunately, he injured his knee during his senior year in high school, and we could never get him in the condition that we wanted him in. Every time we tried to practice, his knee puffed up. It was just a crime. But John Ray was as easy-going and friendly as any player on our team. He was another West Virginia guy who loved the Mountaineers.

REGGIE REMBERT

Reggie Rembert was the best deep threat we ever had at wide receiver. At the time, we were playing the option passing game. He was running a lot of post patterns off the option. Reggie made some great catches on long balls. Major would heave them up, and Reggie would run underneath them. It's a shame he listened to the wrong people when he got to pro football, because he could have had a great career there.

TODD SAUERBRUN

Todd Sauerbrun is a free spirit, but he was a great punter for us. He's still one of the top punters in NFL ten years later. I never saw a kid who could launch a football like he can. He just knows how to punt, and he was sensational on kickoffs, too. He's a real athlete. He was an All-America lacrosse player in high school, and when he was our punter, he wanted to be on the kickoff teams. He wanted to hit.

FRED SMALLS

When we recruited Fred Smalls, he was a disaster waiting to happen, but our football and discipline program got him going in the right direction, and he turned out to be a whale of a linebacker. As good as he was a player, he's now a part-time minister, a businessman, and a great family guy. That's what coaching is all about. It's not just about Darryl Talley playing 15 years in the pros; it's about guys who take advantage of football to become great citizens and great people. I can't even remember all the games we won and lost, but I'll always remember a guy like Freddy Smalls.

GARY STILLS

Our football program did an awful lot for Gary Stills, and he did an awful lot for us. He was a great pass rusher, quick as a cat, and gave 110 percent on every play. Gary had a crazy sense of humor, but on the football field he was all business. No matter how many injuries he had, we'd always have to drag him off the field. He's one of the smaller linebackers in the NFL, but he's been there seven years because of his effort and the way he plays special teams.

DARREN STUDSTILL

Darren Studstill was unselfish in tough situations. He was an excellent quarterback. Heavens, he's as responsible as anybody for our '93 team going 11-0. Darren had mental toughness and quite a knack for being ready to turn it on at any moment. When you put him in, he was ready to go. He was a very talented quarterback with great values, and a great family. There's nobody better.

DARRYL TALLEY

Darryl Talley was not a real big guy at outside linebacker, but he was quick as a cat. He was a nasty young guy on that field—he came to play. He took to our coaching and discipline programs when we came to West Virginia and got a lot stronger and faster. We did an awful lot of things with Darryl because of his abilities, bringing him from the outside and also playing him some at corner in what we called a tough coverage. He was amazing when we played a really good Maryland team in 1982. We were up by one point, and they went for two so we brought Darryl off the corner. The quarterback turned around, and their tight end was running open going across when Darryl about killed that quarterback and saved the victory for us. Darryl Talley turned out to be one of the greatest players we ever had.

JOHN THORNTON

John Thornton was a special find for us. Thunder wasn't highly recruited, but he was a big athlete. His attitude was really good, and it was contagious to our team. Once he got his confidence, he believed he could do anything. As defensive linemen go, he's got to be as good as we ever had. Thunder played inside for us, and the opposing team always had to put two guys to block him, and that freed up a linebacker for us. He was a dominant force inside; no one could block him.

RENALDO TURNBULL

Renaldo Turnbull came to us from the Virgin Islands. He played eight-man football and ran on the track team. We knew he had potential. When Renaldo came for his recruiting visit, he was standing on our sidelines during a night game in which we beat Penn State. Renaldo had never seen more than 300 people at a football game before, so he was ready to sign. We didn't have a clue if he was a tight end, a linebacker, or what. We didn't know what he was, except he was about 6'5" and could run like a deer. We got ourselves a heck of a football player and a smart guy who has done well in business since he retired from the pros.

MIKE VANDERJAGT

To be honest, we thought that we had a great punter and a pretty darn good quarterback in Mike Vanderjagt. He was a Canadian guy who came to us from junior college. We recruited Vanderjagt as a punter and at the same time, we recruited Todd Sauerbrun as a kicker. We soon found out that we needed to switch them. I told Donnie Young, "Let's not tell anybody about this one." Mike was one heck of an athlete. Mike really wanted to be a pro, so he went back to Canada and played up there for a few years, then came to the NFL. He just worked and worked at it. Now he's the most accurate kicker in NFL history.

DARRELL WHITMORE

Darrell Whitmore was a great football player as well as a great baseball player. Unfortunately, Darrell broke his leg in the final game of '88 (his freshman year), and that really hurt us for the Fiesta Bowl. I made a mistake as a coach by changing positions around. But Darrell was a tremendous athlete who made it look easy. He was a big-time free safety, as well as a big guy with a smile that lights up a room.

GRANT WILEY

When I redshirted Grant Wiley, I knew he was going to be a very special football player—10 times better than we ever thought he would be when we recruited him. When he came to our camp, we fell in love with this guy, but it wasn't until we saw him on the scout teams that we knew we had something special. He started as a redshirt freshman and was the Big East rookie of the year. After I retired, I loved to sit up in the stands and watch him play. He was just sensational.

PAUL WOODSIDE

Paul Woodside was the most contagious football player I ever had in the 21 years that I coached at WVU. I think that he did as much, or more, for the teams he was on than any other player I ever had, and he did it all as the kicker. Paul was super at what he did, but he was the team jokester and clown, so it took on a whole new personality. The referee at the Peach Bowl came up to me and said, "Coach, that kicker of yours is unbelievable." I said, "Oh, I know." I was thinking he was talking about the way that Woody had made four field goals in that game. But the referee said, "You know what he said to me? When he came out on the field for his fourth field goal, he turned around to me and said, 'We've got to quit meeting like this.'" Woody was just a freshman then, but he never lost that humor.

AMOS ZEREOUE

Amos Zereoue had so much God-given talent: strength, physicalness, and power. He was so strong naturally, and he had a good work ethic off the field, but practice wasn't always his favorite thing. However, he was tireless in a game. The tougher the game got, the tougher Amos got. He was very serious, and intense—he didn't monkey around in a game. He was a great back, and held almost all our records in just three years. If he hadn't left early, he would probably have all our records for years to come.

It gets redundant to say, "This guy is special," but all of these guys really were.

11

CAPTAINS

VOTING

Choosing captains was a big deal—just how I thought it should be. Captains were picked by a team vote—every player and coach had a vote. I always felt that the players knew who their leaders were better than anyone else, and being voted as captain by your teammates made the role a tremendous honor.

The vote would take place at the end of our preseason camp. In the week or so before that, each of the seniors had a chance to talk to the team and explain what their goals for the season were. These weren't campaign speeches, they were merely a way for the team to know what mattered most to the seniors.

My administratior Mike Kerin collected the ballots, and I counted the votes. We usually picked one guy from offense and one guy from the defense; sometimes I was surprised by the names that emerged. After the votes were counted, the entire team went out into the stadium where the marching band would put on a show for us. West Virginia has one of the premier marching bands in America, and I wanted the football team to be able to enjoy them. It also gave us a chance as a team to let the band know how much we appreciated what they did for our state and our fans.

The band would go through the entire pregame show, and then we would list the football team's goals on the scoreboard. Next, the names of the seniors would flash across the scoreboard one by one, and at the end, the captains would be listed. There would always be a big cheer for the new captains. That selection procedure never changed in my 21 seasons at West Virginia.

1980

I think that the position was extra special for the captains of the 1980 team, because they were starting something off. The first captains were Gordon Gordon (just his name still makes me smile), and Fulton Walker. Gordon was an offensive lineman from Moundsville. I never thought I would have a tobacco-chewing, truck-driving captain, but he was a great one. He was highly respected by all of the guys on the team. Fulton, who played in the secondary and on returns, was from Martinsburg, West Virginia. He had natural ability. Those two guys epitomized that "willing to try" attitude that built a great foundation for Mountaineer football.

1981

Oliver Luck, quarterback, was our offensive captain. He was a dream-come-true type of guy. He was brilliant in the classroom and could swing with anyone—he could be just as happy hanging out with the guys in the locker room as he was in going to the Governor's Mansion or meeting the President of the United States. Ollie has done a lot since West Virginia—the NFL, law school,

Oliver Luck (QB from 1980-81) is truly one of a kind.

running the NFL European league, working in international business, and now a key part of the city sports management in Houston—but he is still the same old, down-to-earth guy every time this old coach sees him.

The defensive captain was Calvin Turner, a big defensive tackle who came from Fairmont. Being captain of the Mountaineers really meant a lot to him, because he was an in-state guy. He was one of those guys who really wanted to see this program succeed.

1982

The captains in 1982 were Mark Raugh and Darryl Talley. Raugh was the best tight end that I've seen for his size. He blocked as well as Tony Becht and caught the ball better than any of them.

Darryl Talley—that name speaks for itself. The team followed Darryl because they knew he was going to get the job done. No matter what it was, Darryl focused on completing it. That focus earned him All-America honors at linebacker, but it also made him a legend to the guys who played with him. He's got a mean streak on the field, but a good heart off it. When someone can start 10 years or more in the NFL like Darryl did, you know that he is a special breed.

1983

The 1983 captains were Jeff Hostetler, quarterback, and Dave Oblak, nose guard. When Jeff transferred here from Penn State, the team didn't realize what he could do for our program, but after a year, they believed in him and would follow him anywhere. He wasn't a vocal guy, but the guys really respected him. Dave was an undersized nose guard who would really get after it with the team. He could shake the rafters, and our kids just loved him. He also commanded a great deal of respect from our guys, because he played with injuries week after week.

1984

The 1984 captains were Ron Wolfley, Dave Preston, and Tom Bowman. Ronnie came here from Buffalo as a tailback, but we moved him to fullback. He loved to play smash-mouth football and turned out to be one of our best blockers ever at that position. Dave Preston was an unbelievable leader as a linebacker. When Dave was a true freshman, he replaced starter John Garcia, who was pulled for injuries. He was in the lineup for four years. He's just a gem of a guy.

Tommy Bowman, out of Portsmouth, Ohio, was one of the most highly recruited kids West Virginia had during my first five or six years. Unfortunately, injuries kept him from performing to his true potential, but he never gave up. His spirit was infectious with our team. He was the catalyst of our special teams. I'll always remember Tommy and the 1982 game when we beat Boston College and Doug Flutie. The game was tied 13-13 with about two minutes to go; we had the ball on our own 36, and it was fourth-and-three.

I was thinking, "If we punt it, maybe we'll get it back, because our defense is playing really well. Or then, maybe we won't, and Boston College will score again, and then it will be too late." The whole time that I was thinking, the clock was running down and the crowd was chanting for me to go for it.

Tommy came up to me and said, "Coach, if you punt it, I'll get it back. I guarantee you I'll get it." The rest of the team heard him say it, and I had to decide.

So I sent out the punt team, and the booing started immediately. We got off a good punt, high, and their guy caught it on about the 10. But Tommy Bowman was right there waiting for that ball to hit that kid in the chest, and as soon as it did, he cracked him. The ball flew loose and we recovered and then scored a couple of plays later. Our kids went crazy because it happened just how Tommy had said it would.

1985

Brian Jozwiak and Fred Smalls were our captains in 1985. Brian had a tough senior year. He was a consensus preseason All-America pick that year, but his hip kept bothering him the whole season. He was drafted in the first round by Kansas City off his junior-year performance, but his hip never came around. His pro career only lasted a few years, which was a real shame.

Fred Smalls was just a ball of energy and enthusiasm. He is a guy who came from nowhere and made it somewhere. Freddy has told me many times that without football, he would probably be dead now. After he left West Virginia, he was critically injured while trying to stop a drug deal. Regardless, he has done well for himself and has a beautiful family. In my opinion, a guy like Freddy Smalls is what this game is all about.

Our third captain was Van Richardson, a linebacker with a big motor. He was a whale of a player from Pittsburgh. His brother Wes played for us a few years later. I think that it speaks well for any program when a player has a good enough experience that he encourages his family to come as well.

1986

John Holifield and Jeff Lucas were captains in 1986. Holifield was a walk-on tailback from Michigan who had a whale of a scrimmage his freshman year in our spring game. He became a very productive back for us. Jeff Lucas was from Hackensack, New

Jersey. He was a big catch at that stage in our program. He was a big guy with good speed, and was sold along the defensive line.

1987

In 1987, Brad Hunt was the captain of our defense. He was a West Virginia kid, from Ripley, and everyone in his family was a Mountaineer. His type of pride isn't something you can just manufacture. Had he not blown out his knee, I think he would have done well in the pros. Harvey Smith, a little skinny guy from Monroeville, was an unknown when he came to us, but he turned out to be a whale of a receiver.

1988

Of course, 1988 was a great season, and that was reflected in our captains, four great guys: Kevin Koken, Bo Orlando, Robert Pickett, and John Stroia. The seniors on that team were outstanding, but those four guys gave a great team the leadership it needed to put together an undefeated season.

Koken and Stroia were both Ohio guys and offensive linemen. I don't think we've ever had two better young men in our program, and they were terrific leaders. We brought Bobby Pickett, a dynamite linebacker, up from Miami. He only weighed 190 pounds in high school, but he could really hit. Bo Orlando led our secondary and was a tremendous, tenacious player. He had the talent and the heart to be successful at anything. He even went on to play in the NFL for quite a while.

1989

We had Chris Haering and Renaldo Turnbull as our defensive captains, and Adrian Moss as our offensive captain for the 1989 season. Chris Haering was a smart linebacker who really knew football. He worked so hard and he led the team by example. He really loves football, and that is probably why he's been such a successful high school coach. Adrian Moss was a big, good-looking tight end. He was a quiet guy who again led by example.

Renaldo Turnbull came from the Virgin Islands, where they played eight-man football. One of our basketball coaches, Bobby Joe Smith, spotted him while he was down there recruiting. Renaldo was six feet, four inches, 210, and could run like the devil. We didn't know if he could play football—there was no point in even trying to watch film on him, because their football was so primitive—but he was smart, big and quick, so it was worth taking a chance. Five years later, he was our captain, an All-America pass rusher, and then a first-round draft pick.

1990

In 1990, the team voted Rico Tyler, Dale Wolfley, Jim Gray, and Sam Wilson as captains. Rico had as big a personality as any player I have ever coached. Fullback isn't usually a leadership position, but Rico really tried to keep the team going. Dale Wolfley was an offensive guard and the brother of Ron, one of our earlier captains. Dale didn't talk much, but he was a tireless worker, especially in the weight room. Jim Gray was a big defensive lineman. He was elected captain in his junior year, the first time that had happened. Sam Wilson was a defensive back who had come to us from junior college. It was also unusual for a junior college guy to be elected captain.

1991

The 1991 captains, Steve Grant and John Ray, were another set of terrific leaders. Steve was a monster of a linebacker and an outstanding player. He was a soft-spoken guy off the field and came from tough beginnings in Miami. However, during his sophomore year, Steve got involved with the Fellowship of Christian Athletes and it changed his life. He is still involved in the ministry and gives inspirational speeches today.

John Ray had more natural athletic talent than practically any of our offensive linemen ever, but he had bad knees. Every time he would play, even practice, his knees would blow up so bad that we had to sit him out. It was very tough for him to get into condition. My college roommate, Ron Blackledge, coached John in the pros and said he would have been the best lineman in the NFL if he would have had two good knees. What a crime! He was quite an athlete and so popular—a home state guy from Charleston—but he got injured when he was young, and it just screwed up his career.

1992

The 1992 team was the most unlucky football team that I ever coached, but we had some wonderful captains: Mike Compton, Lorenzo Styles, Boris Graham, and Rick Dolly. Compton was a peach of a guy, maybe the best center on any of my teams. He was an academic All-American, as well as a busy as a husband and father while he was at West Virginia. He was a finalist for the Lombardi Award and spoke at the NCAA convention. Lorenzo Styles, from Miami, was his best buddy; whenever you saw one, you saw the other. It was like somebody pressed them together into one guy.

Lorenzo was black and from the city, while Mike was white and from the country, but they were exactly like brothers. They competed like brothers do, which made both of them better. If Lorenzo lifted 450, then Mike would try to beat him. If Mike finished a drill fast, then Lorenzo would try to beat his time. Their friendly competition rubbed off on the team in an extremely positive way.

Dolly was a defensive lineman, a West Virginia guy from over at Keyser, who just loved being a Mountaineer. At one point, he was playing with a big cast on a broken hand, but we had so many injuries that he couldn't come out of the game. Graham was hit by a million injuries, but he never let up.

1993

In 1993, every single thing went our way. Mike Collins, Rich Braham, and Tim Brown were the leaders. Collins was outgoing and full of energy. He was the key cog in our young secondary. He was another West Virginia guy, from Huntington. Tim Brown, a junior college linebacker from up in Pittsburgh, put effort into every play. Rich Braham, from University High in Morgantown, just about popped his buttons out all over when he was voted captain. He was a dominator on the offensive line, and a dyed-in-the-wool Mountaineer who loved this football program.

1994

During the 1994 season we were rebuilding, but we had tremendous captains in Matt Taffoni and Tom Robsock. Those two guys led us to a remarkable run during the second half of that season. Compared to most linebackers, Taffoni didn't have speed or the height, but he had a whale of a heart and that made him a great football player. Tommy Robsock, another of our Berwick, Pennsylvania guys, was the mayor of our offensive line—the kids did whatever he suggested.

1995

In 1995, we had four captains: Aaron Beasley, Buddy Hager, Lovett Purnell, and Rob Keys.

Aaron Beasley was such a gifted athlete—he led the nation in interceptions—but his energy and leadership went way beyond that. Beaz was an infectious guy who made everybody around him play a little bit harder. Buddy Hager was a West Virginia guy who would give anything for the football program, but he was never healthy enough to play up to his potential, and that was a shame. Lovett came to Morgantown undersized and really worked his tail off. By his senior year, he was as good as any tight end in America. Rob was our first captain who played primarily on special teams. He really knew the game and loved to study it. He became a great young coach.

1996

I don't think I had counted even half of the votes in 1996 when the outcome became obvious. Charles Emanuel was a guy all the players on the team just loved. He was so steady in our secondary and a polished guy off the field. Chad Johnston, our quarterback, was the offensive captain. He was from little Peterstown, West Virginia, and was so proud to be captain of the Mountaineers. I'll never forget recruiting Chad.

When Steve Dunlap and I drove down to Peterstown, which is right on the Virginia border, it seemed like we were a million miles from Morgantown. Chad had a basketball game at 7:30 that night, and we were scheduled for the home visit at 10:00. Steve and I went down to the little high school gym and settled into the bleachers to watch Chad play. Well, that game went into overtime—five overtimes! Man, we were getting sore from sitting there! It was going on midnight before we left the gym, and we still had to go over to the Johnston home. That was not a quick hello-goodbye, because Mom had enough food for the whole community.

By the time Steve and I finally started home, we were dog-tired. I told Steve just to get us back to Morgantown as quick as possible. At about 3:00 a.m., we were passing through Summersville (a place where every West Virginian knows to watch his speed) when one of the local police stopped us. When he recognized us, he said, "Coach, what are you doing out at this time of night?"

I told him that Steve and I had been trying to recruit a quarterback. The policeman said, "I hope he's a good one," and then sent us on our way. I might be the only person ever to get out of a speeding ticket in Summersville, and it was all thanks to Chad Johnston—and, yes, he sure was worth the trip.

1997

In 1997, Shawn Foreman was elected captain while he was still a junior. He was a talented receiver and had a contagious personality. The players on the team gravitated to Shawn like you couldn't believe—he was a pied piper. He was a hard guy not to love because he never lost his cool. The entire time he was in our program, Shawn was a highly respected guy.

Henry Slay, our defensive captain, was an awful lot of football player for us. He did a heck of a job up front, and the kids respected him. Leroy White was a whale of a fullback before he ran into the knee problems. Leroy experienced plenty of adversity, but he committed himself to work through all of it and succeeded.

1998

In 1998, Shawn Foreman was a captain again—he's the only guy who was ever elected twice—along with Bryan Pukenas, Gary Stills, and John Thornton. We had a hell of a team that year, but things didn't go smoothly. We opened up the season with a loss to Ohio State, and from there, things continued to go downhill. If we had opened up with Bowling Green, we might have won all of the games that season, but that wasn't what happened. That team was not a lot of fun to coach, but our captains were outstanding guys and dynamite players.

Bryan Pukenas was from Holy Cross in New Jersey. He was a super lineman who later went to med school. John Thornton, who has proven to be a great defensive lineman in the pros, was a silent guy when he first came to Morgantown. He was a skinny tight end from a little school in the Pennsylvania countryside. After his sophomore year, he gained confidence and became vocal. By his senior year, he was the leader of not just the defense, but of the entire team. Gary Stills, on the other hand, came to Morgantown full of confidence. Gary wasn't a big guy, but he was quick as could be and all gristle—a great defender. On the field, he would get after all of the guys, but off it, he was as likeable as anyone on our team.

1999

Our 1999 captains were Anthony Becht, Marc Bulger, and Barrett Green, and all three of them are still in the NFL. Tony Becht came out of nowhere to become a great tight end. The only other scholarship he was offered was to an I-AA school near his hometown.

When Tony came to Morgantown, he was about 6 feet, 4 inches, and 198 pounds, but he built himself up. He was just a highly respected and talented guy. Marc Bulger, quarterback, was pretty much the same as Tony in that no other schools really wanted him. Bulger came to Morgantown weighing only 160 pounds—even my coaches thought I had lost it when I offered him a scholarship. I knew Marc had a quick release, strong work ethic, and I thought that he would fill out into a tremendous passer. My coaches were also disappointed when I took Barrett Green, a

Khori Ivy, Barrett Green, Marc Bulger, and Tony Becht at the Big East Press Day in 1999.

linebacker out of Florida, right away, because he was only 180 pounds. His dad, Joe, was the one who convinced me.

Joe Green had been my captain at Bowling Green, and I had really come to love him. I said, "Joe, how good's your kid?"

Joe said, "He's better than me."

I questioned that, because Joe was a terrific player, but he said, "Coach, he'll knock your socks off."

I said, "Well, who else wants him?"

Joe said, "Everybody wants him. Miami wants him, but I've told them all he's going to West Virginia."

Now what was I going to say to that? Barrett came to Morgantown, and he turned out to be a great player.

2000

The captains of my last team were Khori Ivy, Tanner Russell, Kyle Kayden, and Chris Edmonds. They were quite a crew.

Khori Ivy was just a dream. Not only was he a talented receiver, but he had an ease about him that kept our team steady. He made two or three plays in the Music City Bowl that were absolutely phenomenal—one catch where he turned the defender around completely, and another one-handed grab in the end zone. Khori was a positive influence on everyone, including the coaches (when you're a football coach and you have a guy who does everything right all the time, you do get biased). Khori Ivy was a very special guy.

Tanner Russell, from Princeton, West Virginia, was maybe the worst football player I'd ever signed. All of my coaches thought he was too stiff to play, but his work ethic, smile, and desire to be a Mountaineer impressed me when he attended our fotball camp. Al Johnson, strength coach, said Tanner would have to do extra flexibility drills for an hour a day just to have a chance. When I told Tanner that, he said, "Yes, sir," and he did it. By the time he reached the end of his senior year, he had become a real force to be reckoned with.

Chris Edmonds, linebacker, drove me crazy at times, but he played much better that year than expected. Kayden was a blue-collar guy who came to work every day excited to play football. He really knew the game, and he played his heart out every down.

Being named captain of a college football team is one of the greatest achievements of a football player's career, and I know those guys who were elected still take pride in that honor.

12

1988 SEASON

The 1987 season was crucial for setting the stage for 1988. We decided to start Major Harris, a redshirt freshman, at quarterback for 1987. Although he is still a household name in West Virginia now, at the time he was unproven. It was a risky decision, because our schedule was pretty tough from the start; we opened at Ohio University and then had to play Ohio State, at Maryland and then Pitt. We ended up losing early and had a record of 1-3. A lot of people were getting down on Major and the rest of those football team because of our record, but we kept getting better and ended up in the Sun Bowl after almost upsetting undefeated Syracuse. All of the players were coming back for the 1988 season, so I knew that if the winter and spring were productive, we would be a very good football team.

SEASON OPENER

The 1988 schedule was favored for West Virginia. We opened up with my old alma mater, Bowling Green. It wasn't much of a game; we whipped them 62-14. The next game against Cal State-Fullerton was about the same. I didn't know much about them—I didn't even know exactly where Fullerton was—but my guys were hungry to play. We won 45-10. Those opening games really boosted our confidence. Our third game was against Maryland, a team that was always a tussle for us, whether at home or away.

We got behind Maryland early in the game (14-0), but we managed to pull ahead by halftime, and we won handily, 55-24. I knew then, because we won by so much, that I had a really tough and solid football team.

People were starting to take notice of us, and I was hoping that the team could stay healthy long enough to take advantage of it. A.B. Brown, Undra Johnson, and Eugene Napoleon were great running backs, and with Major on the field, we had a lot of options every play.

THE FIRST REAL TEST

Our fourth game was at Pitt. The Panthers were our top rival and were still a powerful program. It was a test for us, and it sure made me nervous.

What I remember most about that 1988 game was one of the last plays of the first half. The Pitt team ran the bear defense, which was a little different. Mike Gottfried had given a lot of people trouble with it. The game had been both teams slugging it out, and Pitt kept blitzing. They had guys coming from everywhere.

With the half winding down, we called—what else?—a draw play. We split the linebackers, and A.B. went through the gap for a 64-yard touchdown. It gave us a lot of momentum as we went in at halftime. It was especially satisfying for A.B. because he had transferred from Pitt; I know he enjoyed scoring such a big play at Pitt Stadium.

From then on, we were firing on all cylinders, and I started to get the idea of just how dominant we were. We scored 14 points in the fourth quarter, and the final score was 31-10. Not only was it our first road game, but it was a huge game, and it built the confidence we needed.

AN OLD NEMESIS

Then we traveled to Blacksburg to face our old nemesis Virginia Tech, another rival that always had a sellout crowd. We certainly didn't play in a manner that I would consider inspired, but we went home with a 22-10 win. I think that we had been a little emotionally drained after two big games. What still sticks with me is that I remember looking at the stat sheet after the game and realizing that we had fumbled the ball four times and lost all of them. I've always been a stickler for ball security, but I had somehow lost track of those mistakes during the game. That's amazing! We lost four fumbles and still won the game? We must have been pretty good.

TWO MORE EASY WINS

The next game, we were still on the road at East Carolina. We jumped on them early and scored in every quarter. Once again, we ran the football with great authority. East Carolina had been a great test for us to prepare for Boston College coming to Morgantown.

Excitement was building for the 1988 team, and we had a great crowd. The team fed off their electricity, and we scored at will against BC—59 points. Major had a great day throwing the football, and the big play that demoralized BC was our little guy,

Grantis Bell, catching one for 61 yards. Our defense played a solid game, which was important. Boston College never changed much—they're always big, strong, and physical. They don't have a lot of speed, but they'll maul the other team. I was glad when the game was over and our record was 7-0.

BEATING PENN STATE

Penn State came to town next. I'll probably never forget that game. With only 20-some seconds to go in the half, we were up 34-8, and I sure didn't want to do anything stupid on the last play of the half. I called my famous draw play. Lo and behold, as I called it, both of Penn State's corners blitzed. I said, "Oh, my gosh, if this thing pops the line of scrimmage, it could go." They had nine guys running in one direction, and we had Undra Johnson carrying the ball the other way 55 yards for the touchdown.

Going in at halftime might be the best feeling I ever had as a WVU coach. Penn State had been such a powerhouse, and we had beat them only two or three times in 40 years. I said to the coaches, "We'd all have to drop dead to lose this game." That win pushed our record up to 8-0. We were starting to realize that we had a chance.

Usually by this time in the season, at least two or three starters were limping around. I've had a couple great football teams that ran out of steam because the kids were too banged up to play well, or even at all. However, by the eighth game, we still had great chemistry and no injuries. Everything was going well.

AT CINCINNATI

Game nine was in Cincinnati. I was nervous early in the game because we weren't playing well. I was very upset at halftime. I told the players, "We're supposed to be a great football team and these guys we're playing couldn't beat a good Dairy Queen team, but we're out here screwing around."

In the third quarter, we scored 24 points. Reggie Rembert was exceptional in the second half. He scored three times and ran three reverses. He was some kind of a character, but no one could touch him on the football field.

CLOSING IN ON THE BOWL

Then we went to New Jersey to play Rutgers at Giants Stadium. It was as cold as a hoot owl, and we knew it might be a little tougher task than normal. Rutgers had already beaten Penn State, Boston College, and Michigan State. We didn't play worth a nickel, and I was really upset, but we got it done. Bruce Skinner, the head of the Fiesta Bowl, was on our bandwagon at that point. He talked to the team after the game at the gate in the Newark airport. He said, "Get one more and come to Tempe." My guys went absolutely wild.

After the Penn State game, we had become one of the Top 5 college football teams in the country; the only other team that was undefeated was Notre Dame, and Miami's only loss was to Notre Dame. We didn't know if we would get a chance to play Notre Dame or not, but the Fiesta Bowl liked us and let us know that our fate was in our own hands. The Fiesta Bowl was hoping we would win out, because they wanted to match-up two undefeated teams, they liked the exciting style of our team as well as the travel power of West Virginia fans.

"PERFECT"

Obviously, we were under a lot of pressure when Syracuse came to Morgantown for the final game of the season. They were 8-2 and we were 10-0; amazing that just the year before, they were the 10-0 team going into our game.

One thing that sticks out in my mind is that after that 1987 game, Dick McPherson, who is a very close friend of mine, gave me a big hug and said something prophetic. He told me, "I'll bet you with that team you have, next year you could go undefeated." He said that a year in advance, and I hadn't forgotten it. However, it was up to us to make it come true, and Syracuse wasn't going to make it easy.

We were home at Mountaineer Field, on national TV, and 65,000 people were packed into the stadium. It was the perfect setting. The play I remember most of all was Willie Edwards' interception and 49-yard touchdown. After that, I had said, "We're going to win this football game." When the game ended at 31-9, the scoreboard flashed the word "perfect." That pretty much summed up how I felt.

The game was over, but all of the 65,000 fans in attendance that night refused to leave the stadium. The team was in the locker room when administration sent word that the fans wanted them to come back out. I told the players, "Gang, take your shoulder pads off. We're going to go back out and run around this stadium."

That lap around that field, running right up against the cement wall so we could shake the hands of the fans, was probably the high point of the season. It may have even been the best part of the 21 years that I coached at West Virginia.

There was a lot of satisfaction in being able to pull off an undefeated season for our state and for our team. There had been so many great kids on that team, and their hard work absolutely blew me away. As the season kept going, we had good luck and great health. We could play the same guys over and over, and they would just keep getting better. However, at about that point, after the Syracuse game, our luck started to run out.

I address the media at a press conference for the Fiesta Bowl.

THE DOOMED
FIESTA BOWL

Whitmore had broken his leg in the Syracuse game. We decided to move Bo Orlando from strong to free safety to fill the hole. That was probably our first mistake, because it realigned our entire secondary. As I look back, we probably should have just played Darrell's backups.

I definitely made some mistakes as a coach as we headed into the Fiesta Bowl. I didn't like where we stayed while we prepared for the game. The Pointe resort was beautiful, but it wasn't the right place for a football team. It was so spread out that it took us two days to find out where all the meeting rooms were, and they were all so far away from each other. With the great chemistry we possessed, our team needed to be together in order to feed off the camaraderie. I was a hands-on guy, and I liked to drop in on every position meeting, but other than the quarterback meeting, I couldn't get to the others, because we were spread so far apart.

Another mistake I made is that I let the media overrun us. I found the attention being paid to me overwhelming, and I didn't handle it very well. I certainly shouldn't have expected my players to do any better. I should have said, "To heck with the press, I'm just here to coach," but I wanted to accommodate them. In addition, I should have put my team off-limits to the media, and just let them play a football game. However, the attention was new, and we wanted to be cooperative. I wanted people to know about our team.

I don't think there was one practice in Morgantown where there wasn't media visiting from somewhere. When we got to Arizona for the bowl game, there was press every day. The players enjoyed the attention, but none of us handled it very well. The prime example was a rap song that one of our radio guys, Tony Caridi, asked some of our players to do for charity. Major, Alvoid Mays, and Rico Tyler were the main singers. The first time I heard it was on the way to work, and it was played just about every hour of the day. I guarantee it was played every hour at Notre Dame as well.

I didn't realize how our people would get carried away with all of the attention, but I'm sure Notre Dame, being more accustomed to the national attention, handled it much better than we did. I learned a lot from the off-the-field experiences during the Fiesta Bowl.

As we prepared for the bowl game, I was worried about the secondary. With Whitmore out, we had made that shift of Bo Orlando, and consequently, many of our defensive backs had been moved into unfamiliar positions.

In my opinion, what happened on game day was unheard of. We had played 11 football games, and not a single person had gotten hurt until Whitmore went down in the last game. Then we went to the Fiesta Bowl, and the third play of the game, Major got a shoulder injury. Major had never been hurt so he had no idea how to handle it. In his mind, he couldn't throw the football and he couldn't run; just the fear from that injury had paralyzed him, and none of us could talk him through it.

This was a huge blow to our strategy. We had basically planned to turn Major loose and let Notre Dame try to stop him—we were scrambling to adjust. Then John Stroia went down, and then Bobby Kovach followed. All of a sudden, we were playing Notre Dame with three starters out, and my quarterback didn't think he could run or throw.

I remember talking to Steve Dunlap and Dwight Wallace up in the coaches box. I said, "We're playing for the national championship and our quarterback just told me that he can't run or throw. How does that strike you guys?"

Maybe we should have just gone with Greg Jones, but our entire plan had been Major, and he was more scared to death than badly injured. Going into that game, I'd have bet my life we'd win, but we just didn't get it done on the field.

THE PLAYERS OF 1988

We had some amazing players on that 1988 team; guys who are still remembered with great affection by Mountaineer fans, and rightfully so. They were a diverse bunch of players who had tremendous team chemistry. The coaches and I always felt that it was a privilege and a joy to coach them every day.

The offensive line was very close. On Thursday nights, they would skip training table to go eat pizza. They were so thick that when one of them got a headache, they all took aspirin. Rick

On the sideline with Major Harris (QB from 1987-89) and Mike Kerin. Major was a player ahead of his time and the most exciting threat in college football.

Phillips and Brian Smider were big timers at the offensive tackles. They were local guys (Phillips was from Parkersburg, and Smider was from Pittsburgh), and they both were terrific during all 11 games. At the guards, we had Johnny Stroia and Bobby Kovach. Johnny was from Canton, Ohio. He hadn't been a highly recruited guy, but his dad and I grew up together, and he turned out to be an absolute gem of a guy. Bobby, another western Pennsylvania kid, worked his tail off in the weight room and became as strong as an ox. Kevin Koken at center kept the whole thing together for us— he had a special capacity for leadership. Of all the linemen, he was the guy who could make the calls and keep the communication going.

We took Keith Winn from wide receiver over to tight end. It was an experiment that turned out better than I had hoped. Winn made a tremendous deep threat at tight end, which was unusual in those days.

We've had a history of great tailbacks, and in 1988 we had A.B. Brown, Undra Johnson, and Eugene Napoleon. Those guys didn't have blinding speed, but they all had good speed and great football sense. We found a tough and very physical fullback in Craig Taylor. Then, of course, there was Major. He was only a sophomore, but he was ahead of his time with those game plans. Major could turn a bad play into a good one. He threw the deep ball very, very well; a lot of people have forgotten how well he threw.

At that time, we did not have a sophisticated passing game; we were a power running and power option football team. If the protection broke down, Major would take off and gain 10 to 12 yards. When you look at today's college football teams, the ones that are winning are doing the same thing—they're all going to the shotgun and using a half-tailback, half-quarterback at the quarterback position, and when the protection breaks down, there he goes. However, in 1988, no one was doing that except for Major.

That offensive football team was very special. We had Reggie Rembert, who was a big-play guy all the way. We had Keith Winn, Calvin Phillips, Grantis Bell, and Jamie LeMon—all of whom could make plays catching the football. We had a quarterback who could run or throw the ball deep, and guys who could run and catch it. It all blended together.

I've always felt that games are won with offense, but championships are won with defense, and in 1988, that was certainly true. Our offensive team was highly talked about, but we probably had the best players on defense. The defense had guys who were physical, tough, athletic, and smart.

Outside linebacker Renaldo Turnbull was backed up by Dale Jackson, and they were both excellent football players. Renaldo ended up being a No. 1 draft pick, yet it took us two years to find out where to play him—he had played eight-man football in the

Virgin Islands, so when he came here, we weren't quite sure what to do with him. However, he had natural speed and size, and he was the kind of kid who would work at it. He turned himself into a great football player.

Mike Fox and Chris Parker were our defensive tackles. Those were two of the best defensive tackles in the history of this school. No one was ever able to block either of them. The other outside backer was Bobby Pickett, and we bounced him around. We put him to the split end side because he was only 6 feet, one inch, 210 lbs., but he could run 4.5. That front five was as good, or even better, than any we've ever had here.

On the inside we had Chris Haering, who would absolutely kill himself for the football team. He was a skinny guy who didn't look like a football player, nor did he run like one. Haering was a natural leader and he was everywhere on the field. He controlled our calls, he changed the defense—he did everything. The other linebacker was a young Theron Ellis. He was almost a freak in his physical abilities, and he loved to hit.

In the secondary there was Bo Orlando at strong safety and Darrell Whitmore at free. Both found success in pro sports—Bo with the Oilers and Steelers, and Darrell in pro baseball. Willie Edwards was the short corner. He was a Morgantown guy who was all heart. Alvoid Mays, who also played in the pros, was wide corner; and Lawrence Drumgoole was a steady backup. Charlie Baumann was a great kicker, and Lance Carion was a skinny little punter who always got the job done.

This team had talent, loyalty, dedication, and great leaders. We were a nightmare to our opponents. The opposing teams had to think we were flat-out scary. The 1988 season was a dream come true and a great testament to the work put into building the West Virginia football program.

Just nine years after I had taken over the position as head coach, West Virginia was playing for the national championship. We went into the game ranked third and played the No. 1 team, Notre Dame. The Irish were an excellent team, but they hadn't beat Pitt or Penn State nearly as bad as we did. It was a shame that we were plagued at the end by injuries. We had the chance to win in our hands, and that's what makes the 1988 season so disappointing.

13

1993 SEASON

1993 was an unbelievable season. WVU wasn't the same talented powerhouse that we had been in 1988, and we were coming off one of our unluckiest seasons ever. We also faced a tough schedule in '93, because it was the first year all the teams in the Big East were playing round robin. On top of that, we still weren't settled on our starting quarterback. It's no wonder that during the preseason, WVU was picked to finish fourth in the Big East.

THE QUARTERBACK QUANDRY

The thing we had to do that season was to find a starting quarterback. No coach wants to have two quarterbacks, but we could not make a decision on who would be the best quarterback. Darren Studstill could do some things better than Jake Kelchner, and Jake could do some things better than Darren. Jake and

The competitive Darren Studstill (QB from 1992-93) was key to our undefeated season.

Darren were both good guys, and the team liked both of them; they even seemed to get along well with each other. I finally decided to play them both.

I told Darren and Jake, "We're going to start with Jake, and play him so long, but then we're going to put Darren in. Later, we'll take Darren out and put Jake back in, regardless of how either of you are playing." At offensive guard or safety, that would have been common, but at quarterback the rotation was unusual, and it concerned us.

Another problem that the coaches and I had was that we needed to replace Adrian Murrell, a dynamite tailback who had graduated. We thought that Robert Walker, a sophomore, might blossom, but we weren't really sure. He had great speed, but he had troubles catching the ball and being consistent on some of the little things. Well, suffice it to say, Robert ended up having a great year in '93.

We replaced All-America center Mike Compton with Dale Williams, a former guard. Dale took to the new position very well. Tom Robsock was an excellent guard. Jim LeBlanc, who had come to us a year before from junior college, was also very good. Left tackle Rich Braham was great. He earned All-America honors before the year was out. Calvin Edwards and Chris Klick got the job at right tackle done.

FINDING THE CONFIDENCE

The first few games helped us gain a lot of confidence. We opened with an easy win against Eastern Michigan and followed up with a high-scoring game at Maryland. Jake Kelchner passed for 270 yards and long touchdowns to Jay Kearney (67 yards) and Mike Baker (40), but the big play on defense was Harold Kidd's interception during the fourth quarter right as Maryland was closing the gap. We won 42-37. The next week, we had a surprisingly easy win over Missouri in Morgantown, 35-3. That game had a couple of big-time defensive plays: a fumble return by Mike Collins for 97 yards, and Vann Washington with a 27-yard interception touchdown. We weren't anything amazing early on, but after those first few wins the guys began to believe they were winners.

FINDING OUR STRIDE

I think the Virginia Tech win was probably the turning point of that season. It had been a close game, 14-13. We fumbled going in once and turned the ball over five times. It came down to Tech missing a 44-yard field goal at the end. Dodging that bullet gave us determination.

After Tech, we played Louisville. That may have been one of the best games of the year. Louisville had the older Brohm kid as their QB and they hadn't lost a game. I was saying, "Oh, brother! What have we gotten into?" It was another close game, but Robert Walker was sensational and scored three touchdowns. We won 36-34. Our record moved up to 5-0, WVU was ranked in the Top 15, but most importantly, the team was believing in itself.

The next game was against Pitt. After a tight first quarter, we pulled away and won 42-21. Mike Baker caught a couple of touchdown passes; Robert Walker gained more than 150 yards rushing; and our fullback, Rodney Woodard, had a couple of key runs. Our defense (Tim Brown, Wes Richardson, and Matt Taffoni, and some great young players in the secondary like Aaron Beasley, Mike Logan, Charles Emanuel, and Vann Washington) was hitting its stride under the leadership of Mike Collins.

SETTLING THE SCORE

I was counting the days until we played Syracuse again. The news media kept asking, "Are your kids thinking about last year's game?" I said no, but that wasn't true. Our kids felt they were cheated in 1992 in the game with that fight. We were in decent shape in '92 until that Syracuse fiasco, and we never quite recovered. Our '93 team was hell-bent to get that one back.

We missed two field goals and a couple more scoring chances in the first half and were only up by seven at halftime. When the second half rolled around, we exploded. The play I still remember was a run by Robert Walker early in the fourth quarter from the Syracuse 10-yard line. Robert took the handoff and bolted 90 yards to the end zone. I'm not sure Syracuse realized what was happening, because no one ever touched him. We won 43-0. That was probably the most satisfying win of my career. I hate to talk about settling the score, but that's exactly what that was.

NAILBITER

Lopsided wins against Rutgers and Temple raised our record to 9-0. At this point, we were ready to host Miami in one of the biggest games in the history of Mountaineer football. We had gained so much momentum and confidence that even against Miami, it was our night. The energy in the stadium was electric. More than 70,000 had braved the freezing cold and were screaming their lungs out for us. That was one whale of a game; a good old-fashioned nut-cutting, so to speak.

The biggest score of the game was Robert Walker popping an isolation play in the fourth quarter for a touchdown. Miami had a great little linebacker who was always running all over the place. There was no way that we could run away from this guy the entire game, so I decided to run our fullback at him. I thought that if we hammered him enough he would finally make a mistake. About the tenth time, the linebacker used his outside shoulder to take the block—that's something you just can't do. Our fullback, Rodney Woodard, opened up the seam, and Robert Walker popped it.

Once Robert got two steps into the secondary, he only had about 25 more to go, and he had burners. Robert sprinted right by the defenders, and all the way to the end zone for the go-ahead score.

We were ahead 17-14 with only four minutes left when we had a second-down situation on our own 35-yard line. We decided to go for it. Jake threw a 40-yard bomb to Jay Kearney that took us all by surprise. Normally, I would have run off-tackle, but I knew that Miami was too good. We managed to drive the ball down to the 5-yard line and let the clock run out. I had been thinking *Do not fumble it! Do not fumble it!*

That game was probably one of the biggest that I've ever coached. At the time, Miami was ranked No. 4 and had the biggest marquee name in college football.

EVEN COACHES CAN BE PROVED WRONG

After the Miami game, I remember telling Merry Ann, "Well, we won the game, but probably lost the war." We were all hurt or sick. The flu was running through the whole team, Jake Kelchner had a bad arm, and Vann Washington was hobbling around. We'd always had great luck against Boston College, but I thought for sure that this was going to be the year that our luck ran out.

From the start of the game, Boston College was beating us every dang way. Our defense was playing pretty scrappy, but we were having troubles with everything else. We were down 11 points with 13 minutes to go and nothing moving, even though Darren had been trying like crazy. I was sure that our winning streak was going to end.

Vann Washington came up to me in the fourth quarter, when the ball was on our 40-yard hash mark. Vann was in street clothes and he hit me in the tummy. He said, "Don't worry, Coach. They're going to fumble, we're going to get it and go down and score." I said, "Go tell 'em to hurry; there's only two minutes left."

I told Steve Dunlap on the headset, "I know Tom Coughlin like a book, and there's no way on God's green earth he is going to throw the football anymore. He's going to jam it down our throat and let this clock run out, so let's bring in Charles Emanuel and Mike Logan at the same time. If BC throws it, the game's over, but it looks like it's over anyway."

Well, lo and behold, they ran it right toward Logan. BC's fullback was blocking the end and there wasn't anyone blocking the corner. Logan hit that kid right in the chest, and we got the daggone football.

We still had 63 yards to go, but Darren hit Mike Baker on a couple of big passes. To score our winning touchdown, we went to what I called our double formation and ran 81. Darren semi-rolled away from where we were going to throw it; we ran a double formation, and he hit Eddie Hill in single coverage in the end zone. Eddie went up and grabbed that ball, and we won that daggone game! That was an amazing victory.

Somehow we got it done; we finished our season with a record of 11-0. To go undefeated with the schedule that we had that year was remarkable, especially considering the fact that we didn't have a bunch of NFL football players on that team. However, we did have guys who were physical and worked at it every week. They were some excellent college players who played their hearts and guts out.

ANOTHER SOUR BOWL

When we got to the Sugar Bowl, our weaknesses caught up with us, causing us to do some dumb things. We started the game against Florida playing pretty well. We drove 80 yards in three minutes, scored on a pass to Kearney, and stopped Florida three-

and-out on the next possession. The next time Florida got the ball, we had them three-and-out again when we ok a personal foul on Steve Perkins. If that hadn't happened, the game might have gone our way for a while.

At the beginning of the Sugar Bowl, Jake was really hot, and I knew it was stupid to change quarterbacks when he was playing so well; however, I'd already told Darren that I was putting him in the game. A coach can't tell a player something and then take it back; he'll lose all credibility with the team. I was talking to Mike Jacobs up in the coaching booth, and I said, "I hate like hell to change quarterbacks. Jake is hotter than a pistol, but yet how can I look at this team? They both got us here."

We put Darren in, and on his first series, he got knocked loopy and threw an interception. Not what we had planned, but what could we do? Florida dominated the rest of the game. That was one of the very few bowl games in which I thought we could have played the opponent 10 times and could have beat them eight or nine of those times.

We had wanted to play Nebraska in the Orange Bowl as the only two undefeated teams, but the bowl coalition didn't like the match. Instead, we were slotted to play Texas A&M in the Cotton Bowl. However, the Sugar Bowl paid more money, so the conference and administration wanted us to play Florida. If we wanted the best chance to win, we should have taken the Cotton; playing a slower, more physical team outdoors would have worked to our advantage a lot more than playing those Florida speed-burners indoors on a smooth surface. But that's all hindsight, and despite that game, what a season! The 1993 team deserves as much praise as any of the football teams in the history of this school. That's no reflection on any other team that's done well, but the 1993 team faced some of the premier teams in this country and played them off their feet.

14

WINDING DOWN

BREAKING THE NEWS

Merry Ann and I had decided that as long as our health allowed it, I would keep coaching until it wasn't what I wanted to do anymore. Over the years, she had some heart problems, and I had some back pain, but it wasn't ever so bad that I couldn't keep coaching. Honestly, I had no idea that I was going to retire. It wasn't until a Sunday night in October of 2000 that the thought even crossed my mind. As I was driving home from yet another full day of watching film I realized that I was going to be 65 years old, and that I had been coming home at 11:30 every Sunday night for the past 43 years. I also realized that I didn't love the job like I used to.

Coaching football is a job that can wear on you. I was especially disappointed during my last couple of years, because I didn't think that the administration was helping the football team as much as they should have. We had great facilities, but they really needed to be spruced up, and I wasn't able to get it done. Mostly, it was obvious to me that my staff was woefully underpaid. Assistant coaches from other teams in our league were making double and triple what my guys made. They would say, "Gosh, we've been around here all this time and look at where the program was and where it is now." I had one of the most talented and loyal staffs in America, and I was sick because I couldn't help them. It befuddles me to think that they didn't get what they deserved. Football camps and such can only go so far, and they deserved better in a lot of ways.

When I got home that Sunday night, I told Merry Ann, "Mac, I'm going to retire. It's time."

She said, "What?"

I answered, "I'd just like to do something different, not football, just something else."

Merry Ann replied, "Well, if that's what you want to do, it's fine with me." The next day, I called up Eddie Pastilong and told him the news.

On Friday, November 3, just before our home game with Syracuse, I called my coaching staff into a meeting and told them that I would be announcing my retirement at the next day's game. Merry Ann and the rest of my family were with me when I told the press about my decision. It was very emotional, but mainly I felt so bad because we had lost the game that day when we should have won.

200 CAREER WINS

A lot of things happened after I announced my retirement. The next week at Rutgers, I got my 200th career win, something only 16 NCAA coaches had done before. That's 10 wins for 20 straight years, so it was a big milestone. However, I hadn't been thinking

My team carries me after my last home game at Mountaineer Field.

about 200 wins, because we had to hang on in overtime in order to win the game.

When Mike Kerin presented me with the game ball in the locker room, the first thing that came to mind was that we'd also had our 100th win against Rutgers. I told Mike, "Thank heavens for Rutgers."

THE LAST HURRAH AT MOUNTAINEER STADIUM

Our last home game was with East Carolina. I wasn't all worked up with emotion. I was more concerned with the fact that we were playing a darned good football team. They still had David Garrard at quarterback, and they had beaten us the year before in Charlotte.

The special scoreboard farewell.

I wasn't sure whether we'd win or not, but we played very well. Our defense was sensational that day. The win gave us the chance to go to a bowl regardless of how we played in the following game against Pitt.

What I remember most fondly about the East Carolina game was how nice everyone was to Merry Ann and me. The television guys talked to her in the stands during the game, and played the tape of a lot of fond memories on TV and on the scoreboard. That was really special to us.

THE FINAL CHANCE AT A BOWL GAME WIN

The biggest surprise I ever had in my life was when we won the Music City Bowl. I remember saying to Merry Ann as I left the hotel to go the stadium, "Mac, hang on to your hat—it could get ugly."

My overall bowl record isn't very good, and it didn't help that while we were preparing for that bowl, my entire coaching staff had been fired after they had been told they had a job.

When we got the bowl bid, Eddie Pastilong said to me, "Do you think the staff will coach in the game?" I told him that I didn't know; they were busy trying to find jobs and feed their families. I held a staff meeting and I said to them, "We've got to play Ole Miss. They've won seven games in the Southeastern Conference, and they've got that big back Deuce McAllister. They're a handful."

The guys said, "Coach, let's just go coach them. We don't want to, but we'll do it."

We went to practice after exams, but it felt different. Those guys were good coaches, they had pride, and they cared about the players, but as soon as practice would finish, they couldn't wait to get off the field to make the phone calls that would land them new jobs.

We were only in Nashville for a couple of days. We had lousy practices and lousy meetings. Things didn't look good. I wasn't sure what to say to the team before the game. It bothered me that this would be the last time I coached them. I ended up telling them the truth about what had transpired; there had been a lot of rumors circulating.

"You know, gang," I told the team, "This is a great football program. The coaches are a bunch of great guys, and this is the last go-around for me. All you can do about any of it right now is just go out there and kick the crap out of Ole Miss." And that's what we did.

We went in with a heck of a game plan that Billy Legg set up. We had decided that we weren't going to play this game like any of the others. Watching the tapes, I had noticed that Mississippi played man-to-man secondary. We put three little wrinkles into our game plan to make it impossible for them to stick with that.

The wrinkles were dynamite. We isolated Khori Ivy on one kid, and gave Khori the entire field to run in. It was impossible for the Mississippi player to match him, and we ended up with two touchdowns. We worked out a blocking scheme so that Brad Lewis would have enough time to throw the ball deep to Antonio Brown for another two touchdowns. For the second play of the game, we had scripted a trick play in which we threw to Big Wes Ours. He rambled it 40 yards for a touchdown. Once we got on a roll, Mississippi couldn't stop us.

When the score was 49-9, our guys were already thinking about the victory party. I told the coaches, "Play them," and we substituted freely. Mississippi did come back some, but we could have scored whenever we wanted to throughout the end of the game.

Ole Miss was a darned good football team, but we had some outstanding guys who had character and heart. Khori Ivy was a talented guy and a real gentleman. Antonio Brown could fly and always gave everything he had. Brad Lewis was a solid, tough quarterback, just like Wes Ours and Rick Gilliam. Tanner Russell didn't have great feet, but his dedication to the program and the University was unbelievable. Our defense—Kyle Kayden, Dirty Davis, David Upchurch, Shawn Hackett, Grant Wiley, and Rick Sherrod—were guys who could hit hard.

I was shocked when all the pieces fit together perfectly that night. I believe our kids liked their coaches so much, that they wanted to send them out as winners.

Paul Woodside (1981-84). My man Woody was one wacky kicker.

LIFE LESSONS OF FOOTBALL

Athletics is a great tool for a young person to learn life lessons. It also provides a chance for a lot of us to chase our dreams and numerous opportunities. Over the years, I've had a ton of people come in my office and say, "Coach, if you recommend one of your former players, I'll hire him."

Just like that. You take someone who's a school principal or selling lumber or bidding construction and he wants a guy who has learned what football can teach.

Number one: if a guy's been a football player, he'll be up and ready to go in the morning because he's used to doing that.

Number two: if a guy has had a tough day, he'll bounce back tomorrow. He understands that when he gets knocked down, he's got to get back up on his own.

Number three: football players know how to work with a team of people. Life, like football, is a team endeavor; individual glory is only possible when the team does well. Good coaches drive that home.

Number four: commitment is very important. Football players work almost year-round—football is a 340-day-a-year commitment. A player is expected to go to school, lift weights, practice, and arrive on time to get taped up. His commitment and passion have to be at a high level.

Number five: football players have met a lot of people. They are put in situations where they interact with their teammates and the public, travel, and express themselves. By the time a player reaches his senior year, he's become a man who knows how to handle himself. A great example is Paul Woodside, our All-America kicker in the early '80s. Gary Tranquill recruited Paul as a walk-on. We needed a kicker, but we didn't have any scholarships left.

Gary said to me, "I've got this kicker coming, and you need to know he stutters—he can't hardly talk at all." On the first day, I watched Paul kick, and I said, "Hey, gang, we had a hell of a year recruiting, and at least we've got one great kicker."

I told Paul that I was really excited about him. He was shocked. It turns out he thought that he was only trying out, so he hadn't packed any clothes for his visit; he really expected we would send him home. Paul called his mom, but he was so shook up that he had a hard time telling her that we wanted him to stay for training camp and she needed to bring his clothes. The guy was flustered, excited, and sweating—it was quite a scene. Four years later, the same guy was doing television interviews and speaking to groups with confidence. He was All-America in every sense. Now Paul runs his own kicking camps and is a very successful businessman. It is because of football that he has that poise.

Attitude alone can help a player grow so much. That was always an important motto for our teams. We wore the lapel pins that said "attitude"—it is that critical to success. When I first came to Morgantown in 1979 I saw a picture of the West Virginia football team sideline at a game and a lot of the guys looked like they were sleeping—all of them had their heads down! I still don't know if Darryl Talley was actually sleeping in the picture, but over the next three years, I never saw him at less than full-speed. He was an All-America linebacker and as intense as any other player to ever wear our uniform. He believed that we could win, and he channeled that energy into winning—all he needed was attitude.

WHAT IT MEANS TO BE A COACH

I heard Billy Graham speak years ago, and he said that a coach has more influence on a young person in a day than the average person will have in a month. Multiply that influence over a year, or even four years. That's why I loved coaching—I was able to teach and prepare kids for life. I realize this even more now that my grandsons play ball.

I always had good teachers in high school; however, I hardly remember specifics about biology, trig, the classes, or the lessons. Yet I clearly remember the games and practices, and how I went to my football coach or my basketball coach with problems. They were the ones who had my attention and trust. They had a tremendous influence on me.

A lot of people ask me, "Coach, do your players call you up all the time?" I think they're somewhat surprised when I tell them no. I realize that my former players have jobs and families to raise; they don't get up in the morning and say, "Gee, I think I'll call Coach Nehlen today." We do manage to stay in touch, and if one of my players had a problem, he knew he could call me and I'd help him.

I got a phone call one time from Freddy Smalls. When Freddy came to us, he came from a bad, difficult situation at home, and we had some tough times together while he was in Morgantown, but we all got through. He called me from Germany where he was playing overseas. The first thing he said was, "Coach, I just called you up to tell you thanks for saving my life."

FUTURE OF FOOTBALL

Coaching is a great life, and I would certainly do it all again. However, I do worry that some guys go into coaching for the wrong reason. Kids see Steve Spurrier or Bobby Bowden making two million-plus a year and they may get the wrong idea. They may think that coaching is easy, and that making a million dollars is average. They may think money is the real aim, and that it's okay for them to take shortcuts to get there. My generation never dreamed there would be that kind of money in coaching football. We did it because we loved to coach.

I'm not opposed to coaches making money, because I know the pressures and responsibilities first-hand, but I think that it may be getting out of control. If agents can get to coaches, they can also get to players. These agents are going to tell these kids, "Your coach is making $2 million, and you are getting squat. Don't you think it's time they paid you $300 a month?"

There's definitely a movement to organize the players so that they get their cut, too. Let's just say that Ohio State is scheduled to play Michigan, and all of the players from both of the teams say, "We're getting the knees, we're the ones getting the broken fingers, we're the ones missing school. We're getting screwed. Well, we're not playing tomorrow." Now what happens? That's a scary situation.

Another thing that bothers me is the way that television has taken over the game. One thing I thought would never, ever happen would be a televised college football game on a Friday night. Now I can watch a college game on a Tuesday, Wednesday, Thursday, Friday, and even Saturdays. Television has taken over football. It decides what teams can play and when. The presidents and coaches talk about the student-athletes, yet we permit games to be played on Wednesday every week. The teams that play are traveling from Tuesday to Thursday. Use your noggin. The kids miss class Tuesday, Wednesday, and Thursday.

Television and high salaries scare me to death. It's becoming a new version of the haves and the have-nots. If you're in the Big 10 or the SEC, you're going to play on Saturdays; if you're in the Mid-American, you're going to play on Tuesdays. Even at West Virginia, our chances of playing on mostly Saturdays are decreasing.

The game is supposed to be for the players; what values they gain needs to be the bottom line. Coaches need to value dedication, commitment, and discipline. A player has to know that eventually he's going to have to pay the piper, and football is a great place to learn that. There are certain rules and regulations teams have called a code of conduct, and if a player can't live up to that, he'll be penalized—welcome to the real world. Young people today need and want to be held accountable for their actions. Helping them obtain accountability is one of the greatest rewards of coaching.

15

HALL OF FAMER

When I got the package about the Hall of Fame last May, I was in shock. I opened up the envelope and the letter read: "Congratulations! You are one of the 2005 inductees to the College Football Hall of Fame."

That's news that takes more than a minute to sink in. The Hall of Fame—wow! To be honest, I'd never dreamed that I would get into the Hall of Fame. I'd always thought that the guys in the Hall of Fame coached at Notre Dame or Ohio State or Southern Cal, and had these long pedigrees. I had been the coach at Bowling Green and West Virginia and was very proud of my record, but I didn't consider that to be much of a pedigree.

That's not to say that I hadn't heard about the Hall of Fame since my retirement after the 2000 season. A lot of people told me they thought I was bound to get in. Other coaches, former players, and WVU's SID Shelly Poe, let me know that I was nominated and when the ballots were coming up for a vote. I found it hard to believe that I was going to join an organization that prestigious, and certainly not in the first couple of years that I had been listed on the ballot.

I don't know how to do much except for football; Merry Ann will verify that. I may have cut the grass a little bit in June, but that's it. Coaching is a lifestyle, not just a job. I coached because I loved it, not because I was trying or hoping to get into the Hall of Fame. However, in the 43 years that I had the privilege to coach football, my induction is the biggest honor that I have ever received. In fact, it's probably the highest honor that a coach could receive. What could be bigger? Only 168 coaches have been inducted out of all the men who have ever coached, roughly 14,000 all-time head coaches. That's less than one percent of all the guys who ever coached college football, and I also have to wonder how many guys never even got the chance to be a head coach.

There were several guys I coached with at Michigan who would have made excellent head coaches, but they never got the opportunity at a major college. The same is true for a lot of guys at West Virginia. In fact, it's probably true for many programs. Knowing that, I have to ask myself, "Why me?" It boils down to luck and timing.

I had given up the best high school job in America to be the defensive coach at Bowling Green, only to have my boss quit only a year later. I was sick because I had to go home and tell Merry Ann that I was out of a job. Luckily, the screening committee for the head coach position at Bowling Green had a lot of my friends on it. I went home after the first interview and told Merry Ann, "If I can't get this job, I can't get any job, because these are my friends." I ended up getting the position.

For arguments sake, let's say I hadn't been given the head coach position at Bowling Green. What would I have done? Chances are, I would have gone back to high school coaching, or to an entirely different field of work, and no one would have heard from me again.

I also wonder what would have happened had I gotten a different job. I came within a whisker of going to South Carolina in 1982. Right before classes had started in January, I told the South Carolina AD Bob Marcum, a friend of mine, that I planned on accepting the job, but I couldn't do it until I personally told my West Virginia team that I was leaving. They all were home on break after the Gator Bowl, and I didn't want them to hear on the radio that I had taken another job. However, the South Carolina university president drove me crazy! He kept bugging me about it and wanted the news to leak out. I called Bob Marcum and told him to forget it. I said, "If that guy can't wait and do things right, then no thanks."

Ultimately, West Virginia was the place for me. I didn't discuss any more jobs after my first couple of years there. I'm so pleased that I was able to make my career in a place Merry Ann and I love so much. The Hall of Fame is a tribute to all the people who love West Virginia football.

IF IT HADN'T BEEN FOR DOYT PERRY

My induction into the Hall of Fame is a dream come true, especially when I consider my beginnings. I'm from Canton, Ohio, the home of the Pro Football Hall of Fame, and a hotbed of high school football where "Hall of Fame" is a magical term. I'm the youngest of six kids. None of my siblings went to college, because there wasn't any money to do so. That wasn't a reflection on my parents, there just wasn't a lot of opportunity for college. I was the lucky one in the family. I was able to go to college because of my involvement in athletics.

I played everything: football, baseball, basketball. However, baseball was my favorite; I dreamed of becoming a professional player. I went to Bowling Green State University on a three-way scholarship: one-third baseball, one-third basketball, one-third football. I played all three as a freshman, same as I always had.

At that time, Bowling Green was small potatoes in the athletic world, but I was thrilled to even be given a chance. When I started school in 1954, freshmen were not allowed to play varsity; we had freshman teams. My dad would sometimes come to the games to watch me play. One game that I remember in particular was against Muhlenberg College. Muhlenberg killed us. The first thing that my dad said to me after the game was, "Don, you picked a good school, because if you can't play here, you can't play anywhere. This is the worst football team I ever saw."

I agreed with him, but I wasn't too worried about my future. It wasn't until Doyt Perry became the head football coach at Bowling Green that I changed my mind about playing professional baseball. He made me see football in a whole new light.

Coach Perry was a real role model, and he commanded tremendous respect. His amazing staff—Bo Schembechler, Bill Gunlock, Bill Mallory, Jim Young, Jack Faust, and Jim Ruehl—was professional and organized. I said to myself, "Wow! There's a lot more to coaching football than I ever thought." He took a terrible Bowling Green football program and turned it all around within a year. Our record went from 2-7 to 7-1-1. The team that we lost to was Miami of Ohio; they were ranked in the Top 15 and coached by Ara Parseghian. After one go-around with Coach Perry, I completely forgot about pro baseball; I wanted to be a football coach.

I was the quarterback, so I met with Coach Perry individually to go over game plans, plays, and to study the opponent; this was stuff that I'd never been exposed to before. All of a sudden, I had an appreciation for the game. Coach Perry taught me about football and how to lead the team. He was such a great coach, and he got me fired up over football.

Off the field, Coach Perry was a great influence, too. At Bowling Green, I was enrolled in the College of Business, looking into accounting because my dad was an accountant. Coach Perry called me into his office one day and said, "I see you're in accounting. Do you want to be an accountant?"

I said, "Not really."

He said, "Then what are you doing in accounting?"

I admitted that I didn't know. When Coach Perry asked me what I wanted to do, I told him I thought that I'd like to coach football. He said he thought I would make a good coach, so he got the papers to change my major and put me in the College of Education.

Later, Coach Perry got me my first job: sophomore football, sophomore baseball, and sophomore basketball coach at Mansfield Senior High School. He opened up the doors for me to get my first job, and I've never forgotten. I was on my own after that, but I needed some help getting started, because people only viewed me as a student. Things are different now—former players become graduate assistants all the time. However, when I graduated, I didn't have any other choice but to find a job right away. If it hadn't been for Coach Perry, I'm not quite sure what I would have done.

Of course, Doyt Perry is in the College Football Hall of Fame—he's the kind of man who is a Hall of Famer. But for Don Nehlen to end up there, too? Wow! I remember telling Merry Ann the night of the banquet in New York, "Doyt would be smiling to see me getting into the Hall of Fame."

Thinking of that means a lot to me.

CLASS OF 2005

The most amazing thing about the Hall of Fame was being surrounded by great players and coaching legends. It's quite an experience for anyone who's ever been a football fan.

Hall of Famers (left to right) back row: me, Paul Wiggin, Jim Houston, David Williams, Tom Curtis, Keith Dorney, and Mark May. Front row: Roosevelt Leaks, Joe Washington, Anthony Davis, Cornelius Bennett, Coach Pat Dye, and John Huarte.

It was very pleasing for me to go into the Hall of Fame with a guy like Pat Dye. He's been a lot of places, but he's always been a winner. Pat and I have been friends since he was at East Carolina, and I have followed his career from there to Wyoming to Auburn. Pat molded Auburn into a consistently great football program. I have always enjoyed his personality.

At the announcement press conference in New York, I met Cornelius Bennett and Mark May, two good-looking guys and great names in the history of college football. Naturally I was a little more familiar with May, who had been a part of those great Pitt teams when I first came to West Virginia. He was sharp and articulate; a graduate like that really says a lot for Pitt. Cornelius Bennett was a super player at Alabama, and he quickly got me laughing with some stories of Darryl Talley, who had been his Buffalo teammate in the pros. Those two are impressive ambassadors for the game of football. The rest of the induction class was a real Who's Who. I asked Mike Fragale to take a picture sheet in New York and go around and get their autographs for me.

The guy I was most anxious to reacquaint with was Paul Wiggin. He had been a great player at Stanford and later a great Cleveland Brown. Later he went on to coach just about everywhere. I knew him because he was a close friend of Vince Costello, a linebacker with the Browns. Vince and I had worked together at Timken Roller Bearing Recreation Park while we played semi-pro baseball. I wasn't sure whether or not Paul would remember me, but as soon as he saw me at the Hall of Fame, he said, "Hey, Donny, how're you doing?" I was impressed, very few people still called me Donny.

Another member of the Hall of Fame class was Jim Houston, a great Cleveland Brown as well. When I was growing up, he was one of my idols because he was from Massillon. I knew his brother Len through semi-pro baseball, but I was surprised in New York when Jim knew who I was.

I was anxious to meet some of the other great players whom I didn't know. One of them was Roosevelt Leaks, who had been a great fullback at Texas. When I first started in college coaching, I heard so much about this guy. Anthony Davis from Southern Cal was another. Tom Curtis was ahead of my Michigan days but still a legend when I coached there.

THE INDUCTION

The Hall of Fame induction process is really glamorous. Not only do the inductees stay at the Waldorf Astoria in New York City,

My family: (left to right) Dan and Janie Nehlen, Vicky and Jeff Hostetler, Merry Ann and me.

but the entire event is a Who's Who of college football. However, the best part of it all was the fact that my family was there to share the experience with me. Merry Ann's eyes were as big as half-dollars the whole time. Danny, my son, and his wife, Janie, were thrilled with the whole experience. My daughter, Vicky, was really glad to be there. Jeff, Vicky's husband and a former player of mine, has been exposed to many high-profile situations like the Hall of Fame banquet, but he said to me, "You know, Coach, this is really something special."

I couldn't have done my job without the very best of support at home. They share everything that's in my heart. Part of my Hall of Fame ring and plaques belong to each of them.

Merry Ann and I were simply overwhelmed by all of our friends who showed up for my induction. We were delighted to be with Dick and Sandra MacPherson, and with LaVell and Patty Edwards. All of us had been together just a year earlier for LaVell's induction. My old college roommate, Ron Blackledge, was there with his son Todd. Ron had been on the staff at Canton South and had coached at Bowling Green. He coached in the pros for many years following that. There were also many coaches and former players of mine who came to say hello.

FINAL WORDS

A lot of things about college football have changed. One of the things is that graduate assistant programs have become pretty big. GAs work hard, but most of them come straight from playing, and they've never known anything except for clean T-shirts, fancy video systems, and new this and that. They don't get a feel for what coaching is like in less privileged areas. My generation is a different story. We did things that young guys today have no idea about.

Video equipment has changed a lot. Young guys today don't even know about the 16-millimeter and 8-millimeter films. They have no idea what we had to do to come up with the game plan. I remember staying up anywhere until 12 to three o'clock in the morning cutting film, sticking it on the wall—all the 10 traps here, all the 12 traps here, and so on in little rows—and then splicing it back together in order to get my teaching film. Today, every major school has sophisticated digital video equipment with a staff to run it. By Sunday night, coaches now have as much information, if not more, about their opponent as we used to have on the following Wednesday or Thursday night.

Technology has changed coaching tremendously, but the one thing that hasn't changed is how the kids and other people associated with the team should be handled. Great coaches know how to handle kids and their staff. Doyt Perry taught me—and Bo Schembechler emphasized it—that a coach's number-one concern should be the morale of his coaching staff and of his players.

It doesn't matter how good the players are; if they don't want to play, then you've got a huge problem. Along the same lines, if you destroy the morale of your coaches, they're going to be a very ineffective staff. Anyone can eventually figure out how to run off-tackle or how to play two-deep coverage, but how do you keep everybody going in the same direction?

In my opinion, your biggest concern should be making the little people feel involved; I also learned that from Doyt and Bo. Bo would pay as much attention to his equipment assistant as he would to his offensive coordinator, because he felt that both of them were contributing an important part to the program. I always tried to subscribe to that philosophy. My one main regret is that the economy in West Virginia was so bad that I couldn't get my deserving staff a raise. However, football took care of my family; I'd have coached for next to nothing, and I most certainly never expected to get rich from it.

In the end, the Hall of Fame honor was just icing on the cake. I never dreamed of receiving it, but it is greatly appreciated. the induction, the enshrinement, the people who contact you—nothing can prepare you for it. It's just something really special.

Receiving the award at the Hall of Fame induction ceremony in December 2005.

Celebrate the Variety of Sports of Interest to West Virginia Fans in These Other Releases from Sports Publishing!

Pittsburgh Steelers: Men of Steel
by Jim Wexell
• 6 x 9 hardcover
• 220 pages
• 35 b/w photos throughout
• $19.95
• 2006 release!

Tough as Steel: Pittsburgh Steelers – 2006 Super Bowl Champions
by the *Tribune-Review*
• 8.5 x 11 hardcover and softcover
• 128 pages • color photos throughout
• $19.95 (hardcover) • $14.95 (softcover)
• 2006 release!

Myron Cope: Double Yoi!
by Myron Cope
• 6 x 9 softcover
• 300 pages
• photo insert
• $16.95
• 2006 release!
• First time available in softcover!

Tales from the Pittsburgh Penguins
by Joe Starkey
• 5.5 x 8.25 hardcover
• 200 pages
• photos throughout
• $19.95
• 2006 release!

A Chance to Win: A Complete Guide to Physical Training for Football
by Dr. Mike Gentry
and Dr. Tony Caterisano
• 8.5 x 11 softcover • 300 pages
• photos throughout
• Retail: $24.95 • Now Only $14.95!

Roethlisberger: Pittsburgh's Own Big Ben
by Sports Publishing L.L.C.
• 8.5 x 11 softcover
• 128 pages
• color photos throughout
• $14.95

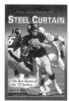

Tales from Behind the Steel Curtain
by Jim Wexell
• 5.5 x 8.25 hardcover
• 200 pages
• photos throughout
• $19.95

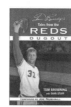

Tom Browning's Tales from the Reds Dugout
by Tom Browning with Dann Stupp
• 5.5 x 8.25 hardcover
• 200 pages
• photos throughout
• $19.95
• 2006 release!

Tales from the 1979 Pittsburgh Pirates: Remembering "The Fam-A-Lee"
by John McCollister
• 5.5 x 8.25 hardcover
• 200 pages
• photos throughout
• $19.95

Tales from the Pitt Panthers
by Sam Sciullo Jr.
• 5.5 x 8.25 hardcover
• 200 pages
• photos throughout
• $19.95